Fodor's
25 Best

SHANGHAI

How to Use This Book

KEY TO SYMBOLS

➕ Map reference to the accompanying fold-out map

✉ Address

☎ Telephone number

🕐 Opening/closing times

🍴 Restaurant or café

🚉 Nearest rail station

Ⓜ Nearest subway (Metro) station

🚌 Nearest bus route

🚢 Nearest riverboat or ferry stop

♿ Facilities for visitors with disabilities

❓ Other practical information

▷ Further information

ℹ Tourist information

✋ Admission charges:
Expensive (more than 50RMB)
Moderate (20–50RMB)
Inexpensive (20RMB or less)

This guide is divided into four sections

• Essential Shanghai: An introduction to the city and tips on making the most of your stay.

• Shanghai by Area: We've broken the city into seven areas, and recommended the best sights, shops, entertainment venues, nightlife and restaurants in each one. Suggested walks help you to explore on foot. Farther Afield takes you beyond the center.

• Where to Stay: The best hotels, whether you're looking for luxury, budget or something in between.

• Need to Know: The info you need to make your trip run smoothly, including getting about by public transportation, weather tips, emergency phone numbers and useful websites.

Navigation In the Shanghai by Area chapter, we've given each area its own color, which is also used on the locator maps throughout the book and the map on the inside front cover.

Maps The fold-out map accompanying this book is a comprehensive street plan of Shanghai. The grid on this fold-out map is the same as the grid on the locator maps within the book. We've given grid references within the book for each sight and listing.

Contents

CONTENTS

3

Introducing Shanghai

One of the world's great cities, Shanghai is China's dynamic window on the future. A dazzling hybrid of old and new, East and West, communist and capitalist, Shanghai is in the constant throes of reinvention. Prepare to be wowed.

The Shanghainese themselves would likely tell you that Shanghai is the fastest-changing city in the world—and that's before the city has properly hit its stride.

A blend of huge size, a vast and densely packed population, a swirl of fuming traffic, plus a here-today-gone-tomorrow approach to almost everything can make this a hard city to get a handle on. The city's commitment to its past (the Bund, the French Concession) and its future (Pudong) creates a sensation of time moving in two directions, while a frenetically busy population of white-collar workers and the industrious middle classes generate a blur of activity that seldom slows. Shanghai is rarely, if ever, unexciting.

But if you slow the pace yourself to wander through the leafy lanes of the French Concession or track down the city's art deco heritage, you can put the brakes on this fast-moving metropolis and sample its more sedate side. And when you are ready for a further lift, you can speed to one of the highest observation towers in the world for extraordinary views over this breathtaking city. If the view across China's city-of-the-future really takes you, some stratospheric hotels offer round-the-clock panoramas as standard.

Shanghai has some of China's top sights, from the Shanghai Museum to the Bund and the skyscrapers of Pudong. And in its quest to blow the socks off other cities in China, food, drink and entertainment have also received due attention. Shanghai's bars, restaurants and nightclubs are among the most inventive in the land.

Facts + Figures

- The resident population of Shanghai is estimated to exceed 24 million.
- The city generated 4 percent of the nation's annual gross domestic product in 2013.
- There are more than 50,000 taxis in the city.

HIGH SOCIETY

Around 30 years ago, the Park Hotel, on Nanjing Lu, was the tallest building not just in Shanghai, but in the country. That seems hard to believe now, when the Park Hotel is dwarfed by skyscrapers. Across the Huangpu River, in Pudong, are some of the tallest edifices in the world. Among them is the Oriental Pearl Tower, one of the tallest such towers in Asia.

ART DECO

Shanghai is a treasure trove of art deco architecture, particularly around Nanjing Lu and in Luwan and Xuhui. Surviving the turmoil of the 20th century, the city's art deco hotels, apartment blocks, banks and theaters are a fascinating roll call of 1920s and 1930s style.

RIDING HIGH

Since 2004, Maglev (Magnetic Levitation) trains have been running between Pudong International Airport and Longyang Road Metro station. At a top speed of 267mph (430kph), the trains complete the 19-mile (30.5km) journey in under 8 minutes. Plans for a 109-mile (175km) Shanghai–Hangzhou Maglev line were reportedly shelved after a high-speed rail link opened in 2010.

A Short Stay in Shanghai

DAY 1

Morning Start with arguably the city's best breakfast in the Grand Brasserie at the luxurious **Waldorf Astoria** (▷ 66) in the heart of colonial Shanghai, then walk along **the Bund** (▷ 58–59) and the waterfront, looking over to Pudong.

Mid-morning Head for **Yuyuan** (Yu Garden; ▷ 74) in the Old Town, then relax over a pot of Chinese tea in the Huxinting Tea House (▷ 70–71, 79) or the Old Shanghai Tea House (▷ 79).

Lunch Aim for the **Nan Xiang** (▷ 79) for servings of Chinese *xiaolongbao* (dumplings; ▷ 66), but you may have to wait in line. Or sample one of the Chinese snacks at the plentiful stalls in the **Yuyuan Bazaar** (▷ 76).

Afternoon Wander the narrow streets of the **Old Town** (▷ 72–73), with their popular dumpling restaurants and antiques and jewelry shops.

Mid-afternoon Stroll through **People's Square** (▷ 38–39) and the neighboring **Renmin Park** (▷ 40–41). Take in the outstanding bronzes, porcelain and paintings in the **Shanghai Museum** (▷ 42–43).

Dinner Have a table reserved on the terrace of **M on the Bund** (▷ 66) for dramatic Pudong nighttime views.

Evening Catch an acrobatics performance at the **Shanghai Centre Theatre** (▷ 50), followed by drinks in a French Concession bar (▷ 31).

Morning Have breakfast at the Austrian-themed **Vienna Café** (▷ 32), before visiting **Tianzifang** (▷ 28) to explore its small shops and appealing *shikumen* architecture.

Mid-morning Explore more of the stylish **French Concession** (▷ 24–25), before taking the Metro to Lujiazui to climb to the observation decks of either the **Jinmao Tower** (▷ 94) or the **Shanghai World Financial Center** (▷ 94).

Lunch Enjoy a memorable meal at **Jade on 36** (▷ 96), in Tower Two of the Pudong Shangri-La.

Afternoon Go for a cruise on the **Huangpu River** (▷ 60–61), passing through the port area as far as the confluence with the Yangtze River.

Dinner Head to **Xintiandi** (▷ 44) to explore the sights and peruse the shops before dining at **T8** (▷ 51), but make sure you reserve a table. After your meal, have a drink in a Xintiandi bar or stroll through the surrounding streets.

Evening Take the Metro to **People's Square** (▷ 38–39) for a drink in **Barbarossa** (▷ 50) and enjoy some staggering nighttime views.

Top 25

▶ ▶ ▶

Around Suzhou Creek
▷ **56–57** Former
consulates and grand old
Shanghai mansions.

The Bund ▷ **58–59**
Shanghai's splendid
embankment is lined with
renovated 1920s buildings.

**Duolun Lu Cultural
Street** ▷ **84–85** A
historic street, lined with
shops and old houses.

Yuyuan ▷ **74** The finest
classical garden in Shanghai
and the city's most popular
tourist sight.

Xujiahui Cathedral ▷ **29**
Catholic cathedral easily
recognizable by its twin
spires and redbrick facade.

Xintiandi ▷ **44** A glamorous collection of shops,
entertainment venues and
restaurants in restored
and rebuilt traditional
shikumen houses.

**Urban Planning
Exhibition Center** ▷ **37**
Intriguing center showing
the Shanghai of the future.

Tianzifang ▷ **28**
Fascinating warren of alleyways, *shikumen* housing,
small shops and studios.

**Soong Qing-Ling's
Residence** ▷ **27** The
home of Sun Yat-sen's
widow is an attractive
European villa dating
from the 1920s.

Shanghai Zoo ▷ **104**
Pandas, tigers and other
creatures in one of the city's
greenest parklands.

Shanghai Museum
▷ **42–43** World-class
modern museum dedicated
to Chinese arts and crafts.

Renmin Park ▷ **40–41**
Pleasant, tranquil space with
museums and a pond, right
in the heart of the city.

These pages are a quick guide to the Top 25, which are described in more detail later. Here they are listed alphabetically, and the tinted background shows which area they are in.

ZHABEI

Lu Xun Park

HONGKOU 81–88

HONGKOU Duolun Lu Cultural Street

Heping Park

Children's Park

Taotong Park

NI CHENG QIAO

Suzhou Creek

BUND / WAITAN 53–66

Peace Hotel

Huangpu Park

TI LAN QIAO

Huangpu

...min Park

Urban Planning Exhibition Center

HUANGPU

The Bund

Oriental Pearl Tower

PUDONG

...ole's ...uare

...nghai ...seum

Square Park

Riverside Park

Lujiazui Green

...Huaihai ...Park

OLD TOWN (NANSHI) 67–80

Yuyuan (Yu Garden)

LAN NI DU

Pudong Skyscrapers

LUJIAZUI FINANCIAL & TRADE ZONE

...nchao ...ark ...tiandi

Huxinting Tea House

LAO XI MEN

PUDONG 89–98

...UWAN

NANSHI (OLD TOWN)

ESSENTIAL SHANGHAI TOP 25

◀ ◀ ◀

Shopping

Shopping is a passion of the Shanghai Chinese. If mainland China has a shopping mall, it has to be Shanghai. From clothing markets and trendy boutiques to swish department stores and mega-malls, the city is at the forefront of the nation's consumer drive.

Nanjing Lu

Nanjing Lu is mainland China's most famous shopping street. While it is particularly touristy in parts, its western section, toward Jing'an Temple, has more style and a larger range of up-to-the-minute department stores. Much of the eastern end of Nanjing Lu has been transformed into a pedestrians-only precinct, which has made shopping there convenient, but this also draws in crowds of out-of-town sightseers. Nanjing Lu is no longer the unchallenged colossus it once was, however, and it has to work increasingly hard to hold its own.

Other Major Streets

Huaihai Zhonglu, in the French Concession, is Nanjing Lu's stylish competitor. North of central Huaihai Zhonglu are several small roads—Changle Lu and Xinle Lu among them—lined with fashionable boutiques for clothes and shoes. Tianzifang (▷ 28) is a lovely warren of alleys devoted to small artist studios, jewelry shops, clothing stores and cafés. Xintiandi (▷ 44) has a popular retail component. The

---

NEW AREAS

More major shopping zones are opening up. The most important of these is on the Pudong side of the Huangpu River. This area has had a difficult time establishing itself, and some shops have had either closed or had to diversify their marketing strategies to cope. However, it seems the continual influx of new residents into the area, and the fact that many of the commuters who work here are among the best-paid in the city, is ensuring its future. The New Shanghai Shopping City and Super Brand malls here are signs of how things are developing.

Traditional shops and markets attract as much attention as chic malls

Old Town's Yuyuan area (▷ panel, below) is great for souvenirs and collectibles. Pudong is home to some monster-malls, but is generally uninspiring for shopping, although this could change in the future (▷ 10, panel). The 50 Moganshan Road Art District (▷ 48) also has a number of trendy shops. More staid Fuzhou Lu is noted for its culturally oriented shops, selling antiques, old books and fine art items.

Department Stores

In addition to individual shops and boutiques, Nanjing Lu hosts several of Shanghai's most notable department stores, shopping malls and supermarkets, among them the New World department store (▷ 48), Shanghai Number One department store and the Plaza 66 mall (▷ 48). Streets running off Nanjing Lu add to its allure, with superior shopping malls like Raffles City (▷ 48). Huaihai Zhonglu also has several top department stores, including Hong Kong Plaza, Times Square and the Parkson Department Store, and Hongkou weighs in with the new Hongkou Plaza development (▷ 87).

Markets

Shanghai's many street markets are both a resource for reasonably priced goods, and even some bargains, and an attraction in their own right, filled with local atmosphere. Some of the best are in the Old Town.

Shop for exotic or everyday items in a rapidly growing range of outlets

> #### YUYUAN AREA
>
> Although the rather touristy area in and around the Yu Garden in the Old Town cannot be considered a shopper's paradise in the way that some of the main shopping streets are, in some respects it is more popular with visitors. This is where you can find no end of antiques, arts and crafts, traditional medicines, souvenirs, and all kinds of minor commodities. Most of these go for reasonable prices—but in most cases only after the purchaser has bargained with great tenacity. The crowds that gather here to peruse, bargain and buy are, if anything, more densely packed than those elsewhere.

Shopping by Theme

Whether you're looking for a department store, a quirky boutique, or something in between, you'll find it all in Shanghai. On this page shops are listed by theme. For a more detailed write-up, see the individual listings in Shanghai by Area.

ART GALLERIES

50 Moganshan Road Art District (▷ 48)
Rockbund Art Museum (▷ 63)

BOOKS

Garden Books (▷ 31)
Old China Hand Reading Room (▷ 32)
Shanghai Foreign Language Bookstore (▷ 49)

DEPARTMENT STORES AND MALLS

Chia Tai Department Store (▷ 96)
City Plaza (▷ 48)
Friendship Store (▷ 31)
Hongkou Plaza (▷ 87)
Isetan (▷ 48)
New World (▷ 48)
Plaza 66 (▷ 48–49)
Raffles City (▷ 48)
Shanghai Centre (▷ 45)
Wal-Mart Supercenter (▷ 96)
Westgate Mall (▷ 49)
Yatai Shenghui Shopping Centre (▷ 96)
Yong'An (▷ 49)

ELECTRONICS

Metro City (▷ 31)

FASHION

City Plaza (▷ 48)
Dave's Custom Tailoring (▷ 31)
Shanghai Fashion Company (▷ 49)

FOOD AND DRINK

City Shop (▷ 48)
Old Shanghai Tea House (▷ 79)
Parkson Grocery (▷ 31)
Shanghai No. 1 Food Store (▷ 49)
Shao Wen Sheng (▷ 49)

MARKETS

Dongtai Lu Antiques Market (▷ 78)
Fumin Small Commodities Market (▷ 78)
Fuyou Market (▷ 76)
Huabao Building Antiques Market (▷ 78)
Qipu Market (▷ 87)
Shanghai Old Street (▷ 78)
South Bund Fabric Market (▷ 78)
Shiliupu Fabric Market (▷ 78)

SOUVENIRS

Blue Shanghai White (▷ 65)
Diao Yi Diao Swap Shop (▷ 87)
Dongtai Lu Antiques Market (▷ 78)
Guo Chun Xiang Curiosity Shop (▷ 87)
Madam Mao's Dowry (▷ 31)
Shanghai Jingdezhen Porcelain Artware Store (▷ 49)
Shanghai Museum Shop (▷ 49)
Silk King (▷ 65)
Silk World (▷ 78)
Spin (▷ 49)
Yuyuan Bazaar (▷ 76)

TRADITIONAL SHOPS

Chinese Printed Blue Nankeen Exhibition Hall (▷ 31)
Duoyunxuan Art Studio (▷ 48)
Huangshan Tea Co (▷ 31)
Lao Zhou Hu Cheng Chinese Writing Brush and Inkstick Store (▷ 65)
Lei Yung Shang (▷ 48)
Shanghai Jingdezhen Porcelain Artware Store (▷ 49)
Suzhou Cobblers (▷ 65)
Zhang Xiaoquan Knives & Scissors Store (▷ 49)

Shanghai by Night

Shanghai is a city that lives hard and plays hard. Its historical position as a meeting ground of East and West has always supplied it with an alluring entertainment scene. Nightlife options are expanding almost daily, and Shanghai is probably China's most cutting-edge city.

Traditional to Modern
As soon as darkness falls, the city lights up as jazz clubs, wine bars, clubs, pubs, cocktail bars and live music venues throw open their doors to well-dressed crowds. And there is a growing palette of highbrow entertainment to choose from, with offerings both traditional and modern, Chinese and international: The list includes classical music, opera, theater and dance, as well as spectacular and artistic acrobatics shows.

Quick Change
It can be hard to keep up with the rapid changes that occur in the nightlife scene. Clubs, pubs and other venues come and go with astonishing ease. Even when an establishment survives, it might up sticks and move to a better location along the same street or to a different part of town. Some nightspots do stand the test of time, but it makes sense to check before getting into a taxi or taking the Metro to a particular venue.

LISTINGS

Several English-language magazines give accessible information about what's on. *Time Out* has a monthly magazine that covers events, things to do, eating out, drinking, the arts and music scenes and more, with an associated website (www.timeoutshanghai.com) that has an online version of the magazine. Also monthly *That's Shanghai* and *Shanghai Talk* do a similar job, with websites at www.thatsmags.com/shanghai and http://shanghai.talkmagazines.cn respectively. Finally, there's the bi-weekly *City Weekend* magazine's Shanghai edition, online at www.cityweekend.com.cn.

*...nghai lights up after dark
...modern pubs, clubs and
...tail bars and traditional
...ese opera*

ESSENTIAL SHANGHAI SHANGHAI BY NIGHT

Eating Out

Shanghai is naturally the best place on earth in which to sample Shanghainese cuisine, which connoisseurs consider to be a version of the Huaiyang (also known as Yangzhou) cuisine of the lower Yangtze delta. Chefs working in these styles have, across hundreds if not thousands of years, added to a rich store of dishes, menus, ingredients and cooking methods.

Shanghai Cuisine

The city's indigenous cuisine has a number of distinctive characteristics. The "drunken" label attached to some classic dishes, for instance drunken chicken (*zuiji*) or drunken crabs (*zuixie*), arises because they are either marinated or cooked in alcohol such as rice wine. Vinegar, particularly the famed vinegar produced in nearby Zhejiang, is another popular ingredient. Sugar is often used as a sweetener, though since it is generally combined with vinegar, alcohol or soy sauce—or all three together—it creates a sweet-and-sour or savory taste. Since the city is so close to the sea, and because it stands on or near to the Huangpu and Yangtze rivers, sea and fresh-water fish and crustaceans form a big part of the menu in city restaurants.

International Menus

As befits its status as China's premier international gateway city, Shanghai has indulged itself and its visitors with national cuisine styles from around the world, along with fusion, world, nouvelle and other fancy variations.

CHINESE STYLES

The city is a rapidly growing melting pot of people from around China. Many have brought their own distinctive regional and even local cuisines with them. There is no shortage of restaurants, ranging from chic high-end places to on-street eateries, serving Cantonese, Sichuan, Pekingese and other major cuisines. You'll also find Tibetan, Mongolian, Xinjiang, Taiwanese, and nowadays even Hong Kong and Maccanese (Macau) restaurants.

Shanghai's restaurants are bursting with Chinese, Asian and international flavors

Restaurants by Cuisine

There are restaurants to suit all tastes and budgets in Shanghai. On this page they are listed by cuisine. For a more detailed description of each restaurant, see Shanghai by Area.

CAFÉS

Dan's Café (▷ 32)
Element Fresh (▷ 51)
Old China Hand Reading Room (▷ 32)
Vienna Café (▷ 32)

CHINESE

57° Xiang (▷ 51)
Afanti Restaurant (▷ 87)
Guyi Hunan Restaurant (▷ 32)
Hong Guan (▷ 87)
Lost Heaven (▷ 32)
Mei Long Zhen (▷ 51)

EUROPEAN

Bella Napoli (▷ 51)
The Bund Brewery (▷ 66)
Danieli's (▷ 96)
Jean Georges (▷ 66)

M on the Bund (▷ 66)
Mr & Mrs Bund (▷ 66)
La Verbena (▷ 96)
Vienna Café (▷ 32)

INTERNATIONAL

Ajisen (▷ 66)
Boxing Cat Brewery (▷ 32)
Brasil Steakhouse (▷ 51)
Grand Brasserie (▷ 66)
Jade on 36 (▷ 96)
Kathleen's 5 (▷ 51)
Ken's Kitchen (▷ 87)
New Heights (▷ 66)
Rhumerie Bounty (▷ 32)
Sasha's (▷ 32)
T8 (▷ 51)
Vedas (▷ 32)

SHANGHAINESE

Bao Luo (▷ 32)
The Grape (▷ 32)

Lao Fandian (Shanghai Old Restaurant ▷ 79)
Lu Bo Lang (▷ 79)
Lynn (▷ 51)
Nan Xiang (▷ 79)
Shanghai Chic (▷ 79)
Whampoa Club (▷ 66)

TEAHOUSES

Huxinting Tea House (▷ 79)
Old Shanghai Tea House (▷ 79)

VEGETARIAN

Gongdelin (▷ 51)
Jade Buddha Temple restaurant (▷ 102)
Songyuelou (▷ 79)
Vegetarian Lifestyle (▷ 51)

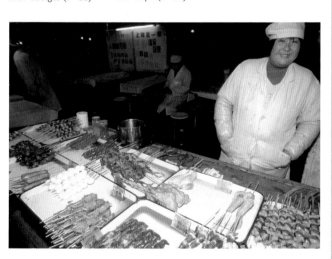

Top Tips For…

However you'd like to spend your time in Shanghai, these top suggestions should help you plan your ideal visit. Each sight or listing has a fuller write-up elsewhere in the book.

INTERNATIONAL SHOPPING

Head for Xintiandi (▷ 44) and its trendy boutique shopping.
Isetan (▷ 48) offers department-store class, Japanese style.
For Western eatables and other products, visit City Shop (▷ 48).
Browse through the warren of small shops and boutiques at Tianzifang (▷ 28).

Shopping in Xintiandi (above and top)

TRADITIONAL SHOPPING

Choose from special Chinese teas and tea-pots at Huangshan Tea Co (▷ 31).
Shanghai Jingdezhen Porcelain Artware Store (▷ 49) sells fine ceramics from the famed Jingdezhen kilns southwest of Shanghai, in Jiangxi Province.
Shop for hand-embroidered silk slippers at Suzhou Cobblers (▷ 65).
Pick up traditional blue-and-white Chinese clothing at the Chinese Printed Blue Nankeen Exhibition Hall (▷ 31).

LOCAL CUISINE

The Grape (▷ 32) serves superb Shanghai and Yangzhou cuisine in the setting of a former Orthodox church.
Bao Luo (▷ 32) provides plain but authentic Shanghai food.
Singe your taste buds devouring spicy Hunan cuisine at the Guyi Hunan Restaurant (▷ 32).
Indulge in a modern take on Shanghai cuisine at the stylish Lynn restaurant (▷ 51).

Chinese tea (above right); a tasty local dish (right)

The art deco Peace Hotel (below)

CHARACTER HOTELS

The Peace Hotel (▷ 62) is one of the outstanding colonial-era buildings on the Bund.
Mansion Hotel (▷ 111), in the French Concession, is steeped in the memories of Shanghai's 1930s gangster heyday.
Astor House Hotel (▷ 63, 110) dates from the early 19th century and bursts with character.
Ruijin Guest House (▷ 111) comprises 1920s red-brick villas in a stunning setting with balconies overlooking its walled Japanese garden.
Swathe yourself in luxury in the seductive interior of the Pudi Boutique Hotel in the best part of the French Concession (▷ 112).

joy a cocktail at a
art bar (above) or
ke in a memorable
robatics show (below)

HOT AND COOL

Soak up the sights of Pudong's spectacular skyline from the rooftop Sir Elly's Terrace (▷ 65), the Bund's largest terrace.
At Bar Rouge (▷ 65) the well-prepared cocktails are followed by well-crafted DJ sounds.
Get into the groove with top international DJs on one of Shanghai's largest dance floors at Myst (▷ 50).
Glamour Bar (▷ 65): The name says it all—a glamorous bar, with a great position at the Bund.

ENTERTAINMENT

Cathay Theatre (▷ 31) offers the best Chinese and international cinema in a 1930s art deco gem of a building.

Shanghai Symphony Hall (▷ 31) is the striking new home of the Shanghai Symphony Orchestra.
Shanghai Conservatory of Music (▷ 31) is a wonderful venue for classical music, both Chinese and Western.
Shanghai Centre Theatre (▷ 50) is the place for enjoying mind-spinning acrobatics performances.

Fuyou Market and Longhua Temple (below)

LOOKING FOR A BARGAIN

Etour Youth Hostel (▷ 109) is a handy and well-presented hostel right on the edge of People's Square.

Café Dan (▷ 32) serves up good-value drinks and snacks in one of Tianzifang's alleys.

Ajisen (▷ 66) offers diners excellent bowls of spicy Japanese noodles, a photo menu and brisk service.

Shanghai Museum (▷ 42–43) is China's very best museum and it's currently free to visit.

The Bund (▷ 58–59) is Shanghai's top sight and it won't cost you a penny.

SCENT OF SANCTITY

Longhua Temple and Pagoda (▷ 26) is Shanghai's most venerable Buddhist temple and dates back to the Song dynasty.

Xujiahui Cathedral (▷ 29) was founded by Jesuit priests, and is still a stronghold of the Chinese Catholic church.

Jade Buddha Temple (▷ 102–103) is China's best-known Buddhist Temple.

COLONIAL AIRS AND GRACES

Not everything in the French Concession (▷ 24–25) is French, but enough francophone architecture, parks and broad boulevards survive to give the idea of a certain prewar *je ne sais quoi*.

Soong Qing-Ling's Residence (▷ 27), a 1920s European-style villa, was home to the wife of the founder of modern China, Sun Yat-sen.

Sit down to a meal or a drink at Sasha's (▷ 32) and surround yourself in its historic villa charms.

The popular terrace outside Sasha's bar (right) and a wall painting (above right) in the French Concession

The stylish French Concession ranges from art deco apartment blocks, *shikumen* architecture and *lilong* alleys to trendy boutiques, chic restaurants and European-style, tree-shaded streets.

YAN'AN

Fumin Lu

Julu

Lu

Changle

Xinle

Donghu Lu

Xiangyang Park

HUAIHAI

Conservatory of Music

Fenyang Lu

Shanghai Arts & Crafts Museum

Fuxing

Zhonglu

Taiyuan Villa

Yongkang

Yongfu Lu

Yongjia Lu

Jiashan Road

Moller Villa

ZHONGLU

Children's Art Theatre

Julu

SHANXI NANLU

Jinxian

Changle

SHANXI Lu

Okura Garden Hotel

South Shanxi Road

Nanchang

Maoming NANLU

Lanxin Theatre

Jin Jiang Hotel

Cathay Theatre

ZHONGLU

Astrid Apartments

FRENCH CONCESSION

SHANXI NANLU

Maoming NANLU

Ruijin Guesthouse

Shanghai Culture Centre

Yongjia

TIANZIFANG

Julu

Lu

Changle

RUIJIN 1 · LU

St Nicholas Church

Gaolan

Xiangshan

RUIJIN 2 · LU

Yandang

Chengdu NANLU

Nanchang

Fuxing Park

Sun Yat-sen's Residence

Fuxing Zhonglu

Sinan Lu

GAOJIA

NANBEI

Dapuqiao

0   500 m
0   500 yds

French Concession and Markets

HIGHLIGHTS

● Fascinating colonial-era architecture
● Excellent shopping
● Fine restaurants and bars
● Theaters and cinemas
● Small but welcome parks

TIP

● Huaihai Zhonglu, which slices laterally through the French Concession, runs for 3.5 miles (6km). Three Metro stations—Huangpi Road (S), Changshu Road and Shanxi Road (S)—are dotted along it.

Oozing style and sophistication, the French Concession—"Frenchtown"—is Shanghai's most chic area: a classy blend of trendy restaurants, discerning cafés, stylish boutiques, art deco architecture and European-style villas.

France Outre Mer The French Concession lay to the south of the original British Settlement, and to the west of the old Chinese town. Having grown to an area of 4sq miles (10sq km), it refused the invitation to join the Americans and British in forming the International Settlement in 1863. The French Settlement had its own buses and trams, its own electricity and its own judicial system and traffic regulations—and it added spice to the steaming cosmopolitan brew that was Shanghai. Gangsters and revolutionaries, bon-vivants and

Clockwise from left: Pedestrians on busy Huaihai Zhonglu; a reading room; traditional cloth designs at the Chinese Printed Blue Nankeen Exhibition Hall (▷ 31); the traffic passing along Huaihai Zhonglu; a table set for dinner at Yin Restaurant; enjoying evening drinks at Sasha's (▷ 32)

refugees were attracted to the Concession and by 1930 French residents were easily outnumbered by Americans, Britons and Russians.

Touring the French Concession The heart of the old Concession was Avenue Joffre, today's Huaihai Zhonglu, which is still at least as good a shopping street as the more famous Nanjing Lu (▷ 36). Tianzifang (▷ 28) is excellent for shopping and dining in an attractive *shikumen* environment. Art deco buildings can be found at every turn, from the Jinjiang Hotel to the Cathay Theatre, while other gems—St. Nicholas Church, Ruijin Guest House, the Moller Villa—dot the tree-lined streets. Other standout relics include the grandiose entrance to the east wing of the former French club, Le Cercle Sportif Francais (now part of the Okura Garden Hotel Shanghai, ▷ 112).

THE BASICS

✚ C7–F7
✉ Around Huaihai Zhonglu
🍴 Many excellent restaurants
Ⓢ Shanxi Road (S)
🚌 10, 42, 911
♿ None

Longhua Temple and Pagoda

TOP **25**

The gates to the temple (left); worshipers inside; a carved lion (right)

THE BASICS

- Off map at B9
- 2853 Longhua Lu
- 6456 6085
- Daily 7–4.30
- Excellent vegetarian restaurant on premises
- 41, 44, 73, 104, 864
- None
- Inexpensive

HIGHLIGHTS

- Handsome pagoda
- Active temple

TIP

- The best times to visit the temple are at New Year or during one of the festivals: Birthday of the Queen of Heaven (Mar 23), Birthday of Sakyamuni Buddha (Apr 8), Temple Fair (May Day Holiday Week and October National Vacation Week). There are processions and traditional music.

The ancient temple stands tall and proud, the pagoda towers into the cloud. Willows encircle the river village, streams are reddened by the blooming peach.
From a Tang dynasty poem.

The pagoda Unusually for Chinese pagodas that survive with their associated Buddhist temples, the stupa here rises up beyond the main temple grounds. The pagoda's foundations date from AD977 (Song dynasty), and although the pagoda has certainly been rebuilt many times since then, it retains the architectural features of the Song period. Seven floors and 134ft (41m) high, the pagoda is octagonal and made of wood and brick, with "flying" eaves of gray tile; unfortunately, it cannot be climbed. It stands on the site of another pagoda, thought to have been built during the period known as the Three Kingdoms (AD238–251).

The temple According to legend, the Longhua Temple was founded during the Three Kingdoms period by the king of Wu and Kang Monk Hui, the son of an eminent minister. It is more likely that its earliest construction was during the Five Dynasties period (AD923–979). In any event, the current buildings date from the end of the 19th century, during the final (Qing) dynasty. After years of neglect the temple reopened and there are several dozen monks in residence. The temple and its surroundings are noted for their spring peach blossom.

Soong Qing-Ling's Residence

The front garden (left);
a limousine presented
to Soong Qing-Ling
(right)

宋庆龄
1893-1981

The villa of Soong Qing-Ling, widow of Sun Yat-sen, the father of Republican China, paints a charming portrait of a vanished Shanghai era. A visit here gives glimpses of how the wealthy lived during a vital period in China's modern history.

Soong Qing-Ling Born in Shanghai in 1893 to a family whose business was Bible printing, Soong Qing-Ling was introduced to Sun Yat-sen through her father's connections with secret societies dedicated to the fall of the emperor. In 1913, on her way home from the US, where she was educated, she met Sun in Japan rallying support for the restoration of the republic he had founded in 1911. She became his secretary and married him in 1915. After Sun's death she became disenchanted with his successor Chiang Kai Shek and went to Moscow, returning to help with the anti-Japanese war effort. After the revolution she held a number of government posts and became a useful symbol for China until her death in 1981.

The residence Soong Qing-Ling's home in Shanghai from 1948 to 1963, in the heart of the French Concession, dates from the 1920s. The house, a European-style villa with a pretty garden, has been maintained as it was on the day that she died. As befits the home of a representative of the people, it is furnished fairly simply, although there is an interesting collection of gifts received from a number of eminent visitors, including a carpet from Mao, and a work in bamboo from Kim Il Sung of North Korea.

THE BASICS

www.shsoong-chingling.
com
+ B8
✉ 1843 Huaihai Zhonglu
☎ 6474 7183
🕐 Daily 9–4.30
🚇 Hengshan Road
♿ None
💷 Inexpensive

HIGHLIGHTS

● Lovely prewar villa with period furnishings
● Well-tended European-style garden

Tianzifang

TOP 25

Browsing the shops and cafés in Tianzifang's alleys

HIGHLIGHTS

- *Shikumen* architecture
- Shopping
- Taking a coffee break

TIP

- There's plenty to see so allow several hours to explore Tianzifang's charming alleyways to soak up their old-world atmosphere.

Admire Shanghai's alleyway *shikumen* architecture while shopping at some of the city's most creative clothes shops and sipping coffee at trendy cafés. This small tangle of lanes is a great alternative to Shanghai's mega-malls.

Shikumen style Like Beijing's *siheyuan* courtyard architecture, Shanghai's *shikumen* residences are motifs of the city. A marriage of 19th-century British terrace housing and traditional Chinese courtyard architecture, *shikumen* buildings—tucked away in rows down alleys called *lilong*—are low-rise, with two or three floors, and fronted with an often elaborately carved stone lintel, lending the name *shikumen* (stone-surrounded gate). In Tianzifang (also called Taikang Lu Art Street), many of these *shikumen* residences are now shops.

A welcome escape Not as well known as Xintiandi (▷ 44), Tianzifang has a more small-scale and manageable charm that makes a visit a more relaxing experience. Alleys branch off from the main lanes, leading to courtyards and further alleys with small clothes boutiques, jewelry shops, art galleries, cafés and restaurants. Explore these quaint passageways to find hidden delights, from photographic galleries documenting daily life in China to stores where you can have clothes tailor-made; and studios producing hand-crafted wares. Lane 210 has some of the most interesting establishments, but you can find others along Lanes 248 and 274. For a break, watch the world go by at Boho Café Kommune (No. 7, Lane 210).

The cathedral's ornate ceiling (left) and altar (right)

TOP 25

Xujiahui Cathedral

In a country of Buddhist, Confucian and Taoist traditions that is now officially atheist, perhaps nothing is more surprising than the twin towers of a redbrick neo-Gothic cathedral poking into the sky in the shadow of gleaming skyscrapers.

The Jesuits The influence of Jesuit missionaries was felt in Shanghai from as early as the 16th century. An early convert was one Xu Guangqi, a native of Xujiahui, or "Xu Family Village," which at that time was well outside the original town of Shanghai. Xu, an official in the Imperial library, was baptized Paul. He later bequeathed family land to the Jesuits, where an observatory and cathedral would eventually be constructed. Following persecution of the converts, the first church here became a temple to the god of war; after the Treaty of Nanking (1842), the land was given to the French, and in 1848 a Jesuit settlement was firmly established.

The cathedral The current cathedral of St. Ignatius was built in 1906 with two 165ft (50m) spires and capacity for a congregation of 2,500. The interior includes a number of decorative idiosyncracies that indicate Buddhist influence—melons appear on the nave columns and, along with stylized bats (a Chinese symbol of happiness), in the windows. Outside, gargoyles fringe the roof and a holy grotto has been built in the garden. Severely damaged during the Cultural Revolution, the cathedral is now a busy place of worship.

THE BASICS

- ✚ A9
- ✉ 158 Puxi Lu
- ☎ 6438 2595
- 🕐 Mon–Sat 9–11, 1–4
- 🚇 Xujiahui
- 🚌 3, 42, 50
- ♿ None
- 💷 Free
- ❓ Services Mon–Fri 6am, 7am; Sat 6am, 7am, 6pm; Sun 6am, 7.30am, 10am, 6pm

HIGHLIGHTS

- European neo-Gothic among the skyscrapers
- Idiosyncratic detail

TIP

- Pop into the nearby Bibliotheca Zi-Ka-Wei (80 Caoxi Beilu) and try to get on the free Saturday tours (2–4pm) of the main Jesuit library room—it's outstanding.

FRENCH CONCESSION TOP 25

More to See

C.Y. TUNG MARITIME MUSEUM

http://cytungmaritimemuseum.com
Wander around historic Jiaotong University before visiting this museum, dedicated to Chinese maritime history.

✚ A8 ✉ Jiaotong University
☎ 6293 2403 ⊙ Tue–Sun 1.30–5
⊚ Xujiahui ⚑ Free

FUXING PARK

A private garden converted in 1908 into a Parisian-style park and pleasantly shaded by Wutong trees, Fuxing Park is a delicious spot for a relaxing stroll.

✚ F7 ✉ Fuxing Zhonglu ⊙ Daily
🍴 Restaurants ⊚ Huangpi Road (S)
🚌 24, 36, 780, 781 ⚑ None ⚑ Free

MOLLER VILLA

www.mollervilla.com
Now a hotel, this rather curious concoction of Gothic towers and spires was home to a Scandinavian shipping magnate.

A grand wooden staircase inside Moller Villa

✚ E6 ✉ 30 Shaanxi Nanlu ☎ 5180 1144
⊚ Shanxi Road (S) 🚌 1, 42, 48, 71, 127

PROPAGANDA POSTER ART CENTRE

www.shanghaipropagandaart.com
This gallery exhibits a fine collection of political propaganda posters from the Mao era. It's a quirky diversion and a reminder of China's recent radicalism.

✚ B6 ✉ Room B-OC, President Mansion, 868 Huashan Lu ☎ 6211 1845
⊚ Jiangsu Road 🚌 48, 93, 113, 328
⚑ Moderate

ST. NICHOLAS CHURCH

Just west of Fuxing Park, this 1930s Russian Orthodox Church, now empty, is an attractive feature of Gaolan Lu.

✚ E7 ✉ 16 Gaolan Lu
⊚ Huangpi Road (S)

SHANGHAI ARTS & CRAFTS MUSEUM

www.shgmb.com
This museum of traditional Chinese arts and crafts is in an elegant mansion with a beautiful garden.

✚ D8 ✉ 79 Fenyang Lu ☎ 6437 3454
⊙ Daily 9–5 ⊚ Changshu Road 🚌 42
⚑ None ⚑ Inexpensive

SUN YAT-SEN'S RESIDENCE

www.sh-sunyat-sen.org
The house of the father of Republican China has been kept as it supposedly was during his life, simply furnished in a mix of Western and Chinese styles.

✚ F7 ✉ 7 Xiangshan Lu
☎ 6437 2954 ⊙ Daily 9–4.30
⊚ Shanxi Road (S) 🚌 2, 17, 24, 36, 42
⚑ Inexpensive

Fairmont
PEACE HOTEL
和平饭店

www.fairmont.com

Please take me to:

Yu Garden

豫园, 安仁街 137 号, 近福佑路

Address: 137 Anren Jie, near Fuyou Lu

Shopping

CHINESE PRINTED BLUE NANKEEN EXHIBITION HALL
Delightful traditional blue-and-white cloth designs.
🚹 D7 ✉ No. 24, Lane 637, Changle Lu ☎ 5403 7947 🕐 Daily 9–5 🚇 Changshu Road

DAVE'S CUSTOM TAILORING
www.tailordave.com
A Shanghai institution, they can stitch a suit in 7–14 days (or 24 hours).
🚹 B7 ✉ Lane 288, 1Wuyuan Rd ☎ 5298 0808 🕐 Daily 10–7 🚇 Changshu Road

FRIENDSHIP STORE
www.blyysd.com
Buy fabrics, craft items, and antiques, including porcelain and cloisonné.
🚹 C6 ✉ 9 Huashan Lu ☎ 6258 6310 🕐 Daily 9.30–9.30 🚇 Jing'an Temple 🚌 15, 20

GARDEN BOOKS
www.gardenbooks.cn
An airy bookstore selling books and magazines.
🚹 E6 ✉ 325 Changle Lu ☎ 5404 8728 🕐 Daily 10–10 🚇 Shanxi Road (S)

HUANGSHAN TEA CO
The place to buy gorgeous ceramics and Yixing teapots.
🚹 F7 ✉ 605 Huaihai Zhonglu ☎ 5306 2258 🕐 Daily 9am–10pm 🚇 Huangpi Road (S) 🚌 42, 911

MADAME MAO'S DOWRY
Trendy collectibles and antiques.
🚹 D6 ✉ 207 Fumin Lu ☎ 5403 3551 🕐 Daily 10–7 🚇 Changshu Road

METRO CITY
www.shmetrocity.com
One of the best places for electronics.
🚹 A9 ✉ 1111 Zhaojiabang Lu ☎ 6438 5999 🕐 Daily 10–10 🚇 Xujiahui

PARKSON GROCERY
Western-style grocery store.
🚹 E7 ✉ Parkson Department Store, 918 Huaihai Zhonglu ☎ 6415 6384 🚇 Shanxi Road (S) 🚌 42, 126, 911

Entertainment and Nightlife

CATHAY THEATRE
www.guotaifilm.com
A restored 1930s art deco theater, the Cathay shows Chinese and new international films.
🚹 E7 ✉ 870 Huaihai Zhonglu ☎ 5404 0415/5404 2095 🚇 Shanxi Road (S) 🚌 41

CLUB JZ
www.jzclub.cn
For late-night modern jazz sounds; open mic on Monday nights.
🚹 C7 ✉ 46 West Fuxing Road ☎ 6385 0269 🕐 Daily 9pm–3am 🚇 Changshu Road

EL COCTEL
Chic, brooding bar from the same owners as South Bund Spanish restaurant El Willy, with tapas and cocktails.
🚹 C7 ✉ 2nd Floor, 47 Yongfu Lu ☎ 6433 6511 🕐 Daily 5pm–3am 🚇 Shanghai Library

SHANGHAI CONSERVATORY OF MUSIC
www.shcmusic.edu.cn
Regular performances of classical Chinese and Western music most Sunday evenings.
🚹 D7 ✉ 20 Fenyang Lu ☎ 6437 0137, ext. 2166 🚇 Shanxi Road (S)

SHANGHAI SYMPHONY HALL
www.sh-symphony.com
Opened in September 2014, this striking new concert hall is home to the Shanghai Symphony Orchestra and hosts leading overseas orchestras. It comprises a 1,200-seat main auditorium as well as a 400-seat chamber.
🚹 C7 ✉ 1380 Fuxing Zhonglu ☎ 2426 6162 🚇 Changshu Road 🚌 42

Restaurants

PRICES

Prices are approximate, based on a 3-course meal for one person.

$$$ more than 250RMB
$$ 100–250RMB
$ under 100RMB

BAO LUO ($)

www.baoluojiulou.com
Plain but inviting, Bao Luo serves up traditional Shanghainese cuisine.
🚩 D6 ✉ 271 Fumin Lu
☎ 5403 7239 ⏰ Daily 11.30–3.30, 5pm–3am
🚇 Changshu Road

BOXING CAT BREWERY ($$)

www.boxingcatbrewery.com
This popular venue brews European-style ales, lagers and American craft beers, while the food is spicy Southern US cuisine. Portions are big, so bring an appetite.
🚩 C7 ✉ 82 Fuxing Xilu
☎ 6431 2091 ⏰ Mon–Thu 5pm–2am, Fri 3pm–2am, Sat–Sun 10am–2am 🚇 Shanghai Library

CAFÉ DAN ($)

www.idancoffee.com
Enjoy coffee, beer, wines, and Japanese snacks in this cozy coffee bar in one of Tianzifang's alleys.
🚩 E8 ✉ No. 41, Lane 248, Taikang Lu ☎ 6466 1042
⏰ Daily 10am–midnight
🚇 Dapuqiao

THE GRAPE ($$)

www.graperestaurant.cn
In a former church, the service is friendly and the Shanghai and Yangzhou cooking reliable.
🚩 D7 ✉ 55 Xinle Lu
☎ 5404 0486 ⏰ Daily lunch, dinner 🚌 45

GUYI HUNAN RESTAURANT ($–$$)

If you've had enough of Shanghai cuisine's soft flavors, go for the full-on spiciness of the much-enjoyed Hunan dishes at this smart restaurant.
🚩 D6 ✉ 87 Fumin Lu
☎ 6249 5628 ⏰ Daily 11.30–11.30 🚇 Jing'an Temple

LOST HEAVEN ($$)

www.lostheaven.com.cn
Popular, atmospheric restaurant specializing in the cuisine of Yunnan province's ethnic minorities.
🚩 B7 ✉ 38 Gaoyou Lu
☎ 6433 5126 ⏰ Daily 11.30–1, 5.30–10.30
🚇 Hengshan Road

OLD CHINA HAND READING ROOM ($)

Atmospheric café and library run by German photographer Deke Erh.
🚩 E8 ✉ 27 Shaoxing Lu
☎ 6473 2526 ⏰ Daily

EXPENSIVE OPTIONS

Always check the cost of dishes that do not have a price on them on the menu. Seasonal dishes, particularly those involving seafoods, can be expensive, even on an otherwise inexpensive menu.

10am–midnight 🚇 Jiashan Road)

RHUMERIE BOUNTY ($)

www.bountybar.cn
Pizzas, calzone, and meat skewers is about as exciting as the food gets, but who cares when you're getting shipwrecked in this pirate-themed bar with more rums than you can shake a hook at.
🚩 B7 ✉ 47 Yongfu Lu
☎ 6271 1406 ⏰ Daily 6pm til late 🚇 Changshu Road

SASHA'S ($–$$)

http://sashas-shanghai.com
A rambling, rose-hued 1920s villa is home to this cool restaurant and bar. There's elegant dining in an upstairs room, and snacks in the bar or on the garden terrace.
🚩 C7 ✉ 11 Dongping Lu
☎ 6474 6628 ⏰ Daily 9–6
🚇 Changshu Road

VEDAS ($–$$)

www.vedascuisine.com
With great service and classic dishes, Vedas is probably the city's best Indian restaurant.
🚩 C6 ✉ 83 Changshu Lu ☎ 6445 8100
⏰ Daily 11.30–2, 5.30–11
🚇 Changshu Road

VIENNA CAFÉ ($)

www.viennashanghai.com
Excellent Austrian-themed café with great food, coffee and ambience.
🚩 E8 ✉ 25 Shaoxing Lu
☎ 6445 2131 ⏰ Daily 8–8
🚇 Shanxi Road (S)

The frenetic Nanjing Lu shopping street skirts the edge of Shanghai's concentration of governmental and cultural installations around the People's Park and Square.

3

4

5

JING'AN SI

Lilong Architecture

Yuyuan Lu

Jing'an Temple

NANJING XILU

Children's Palace

HUASHAN LU

Jing'an Temple

Jing'an Park

Xinzha

BEIJING

Nanyang

NANJING

Yuyuan

Anyi

YAN'AN

Shanghai Centre

Nanyang Lu

Beili

Majestic Theatre

XILU

SHANXI BEILU

Shanghai Exhibition Centre

Weihai

ZHONGLU

Lu

Nanjing

Xinzha Lu

XILU

West Nanjing Road

Wulumuqi Lu

SHIMEN 2-LU

Nanjing Lu

Feng

Wulang

SHIMEN 1-LU

Weih

Ruijin Theatre

Jiaou

Square Park

6

7

8

NANJI

Toc Mus

0		500 m
0		500 yds

9

C

D

E

(Suzhou Creek)

NI CHENG QIAO

Xinzha Road

Wusong

Xiamen

Huangpu Theatre

BEIJING

XILU

Guling

Zhongguo Theatre

DONGLU

BEIJING

Niuzhuang

Ningbo

Ningbo

Tianjin

NANJING

Fujian

Duoyunxuan Art Studio

Grand Brightness Theatre

People's Square

Wusha Monument

DONGLU

Nanjing Road (E)

HENAN

ZHONGLU

Renmin Park

Jiujiang

Jiujiang

NANJING

XILU

MOCA

Hankou

Fujian

Hankou

Shanghai Municipal People's Government

People's Square

Shanghai Grand Theatre

Urban Planning Exhibition Center

Tianchan Yifu Theatre

Fuzhou

HUANGPU

Shantou Lu

Renmin Dadao

Guangdong

Lu

People's Square

Wusheng

Shanghai Museum

Beihai

DONGLU

YAN'AN

Gong Theatre

Concert Hall

Donglu

Square Park

Jinling

Zhonglu

Jinling

Dazhong Theatre

Xilu

South Huangpi Road

HUAIHAI

ZHONGLU

Taoyuan

HUAIHAI DONGLU

Xing'an

Huaihai Park

Dashijie

Taicang

Memorial House of the First National Congress of the Communist Party

Chengda Lu

Shouning Lu

Xintiandi

Taipingqiao Park

Zizhong

Xintiandi

Fuxing

Zhonglu

Laoximen

NANLU

LUWAN

Hefei

Lu

Donglu

Dali

Anlan Lu

Dali Lu

F   **G**   **H**

Neon lights (left); a flying-saucer-style revolving restaurant tops the Radisson (far right)

Nanjing Lu

TOP 25

THE BASICS

➕ C6–J5
🍴 Many excellent restaurants
🚇 Nanjing Road (E), People's Square, Nanjing Road (W), Jing'an Temple
🚌 20, 37
♿ None

HIGHLIGHTS

● Heart of workaday Shanghai
● Excellent shopping
● Period architecture

TIP

● Nanjing Donglu can be noisy, with huge numbers of shoppers and tourists. If you want to evade the crowds and speed along the pedestrianized length of Nanjing Donglu, jump aboard one of the fun tourist "trains" that travel from the People's Square end to Henan Zhonglu. Tickets are cheap and trains leave regularly.

Starting at the Bund's Peace Hotel, storming through People's Square, and taking shoppers all the way west to the Jing'an Temple, Nanjing Road is Shanghai's most famous thoroughfare.

The past The name commemorates the treaty that, in 1842, gave trading rights to the foreign powers of the era (▷ 124). As Shanghai grew, so did Nanjing Lu, snaking through the heart of the International Settlement to become, at its western end, the Bubbling Well Road (now Nanjing Xilu), named after a well near the Jing'an Temple.

Today Although rivaled by Huaihai Zhonglu for shopping, Nanjing Lu remains Shanghai's main thoroughfare, bordered in the east by the Bund and the Huangpu River. Nanjing Donglu (East Nanjing Road) is the liveliest section, especially the pedestrians-only strip between Henan Zhonglu and Xizang Zhonglu—come here at night for the neons. Along Nanjing Donglu, keep an eye out for its art-deco buildings, including the Peace Hotel (▷ 62). Other historic buildings include the Shanghai No. 1 Department Store and the former Shanghai Sincere Department Store, now the East Asia Hotel (▷ 109). Where Nanjing Donglu meets Nanjing Xilu (Nanjing Road West) is the old racecourse grandstand, formerly home to the Shanghai Art Museum, its collection now rehoused in the China Art Museum and Power Station of Art at the Expo Site (▷ 100–101), and the Park Hotel (▷ 109), once the tallest building outside the Americas.

TOP 25

Urban Planning Exhibition Center

This fascinating museum (Chengshi Guihua Zhanshiguan), on the eastern end of People's Square, propels visitors into the future by showing them what the city might look like in the year 2020.

What's in a name? They could easily have given this museum a more attractive name, but don't judge it on this basis alone. Begin your odyssey on the mezzanine floor, where a 20-minute film takes you on a whistle-stop tour of 100 years of Shanghai history.

City plans Prepare to be bowled over by the star attraction, a scale model of the city as it is planned to look in the year 2020, so detailed that it takes up the entire third floor. The high-tech displays on the fourth floor turn the spotlight on mammoth construction projects like the Yangshan deep-water port and the Expo Site (▷ 100–101).

Relentless change One rather sad exhibit is of those older areas that are slated for demolition, only to be replaced by soulless modern apartments and office towers. Not all of this will be considered a loss by their current residents, whose wish for more comfortable accommodations will be fulfilled. Yet parts of town that might well be worth saving and refurbishing will disappear, too, and there seems to be nothing to stop the development juggernaut that has already rolled over so many parts of old Shanghai. In partial compensation, there are working re-creations of old shops and teahouses in the museum basement.

THE BASICS

www.supec.org

🔳 G6

✉ 100 Renmin Dadao

☎ 6372 2077

🕐 Tue–Thu 9–5, Fri–Sun 9–6 (last ticket one hour before closing). Closed Mon

🍴 Museum café

Ⓟ People's Square

🚍 46, 71, 123, 574

💰 Moderate

♿ Good

HIGHLIGHTS

● Scale model of Shanghai's 2020 vision
● Top-floor café

TIP

● Take an opera glass or a small pair of binoculars for close-up views of the beautifully detailed scale model of Shanghai in 2020.

People's Square

HIGHLIGHTS

● Shanghai Museum
● Renmin Park
● Grand Theatre

TIP

● For long, long views over the city, take the elevator to the lobby of the J.W. Marriott Hotel, in dazzling Tomorrow Square, or slowly revolve while dining within Epicure on 45, at the summit of the Radisson Hotel Shanghai New World.

If Shanghai's magnificent sprawl has a focal point, this is it. Many of the city's top attractions cluster here, among the swell of museum-goers, shoppers, white-collar workers and out-of-towners.

Bustling hub Redesigned in the 1990s, People's Square—perhaps the most popular name for city squares in China—is the equivalent of Beijing's Tiananmen Square, but is far more accessible. As Shanghai's largest Metro interchange, the square and its environs are constantly flooded with people, crossing over to Nanjing Donglu, doing exercises, flying kites or taking a break.

Seeing the sights The best way to negotiate People's Square (Renmin Guangchang) is to take the Metro exit to Renmin Dadao (People's

Clockwise from left: A small child feeds the pigeons; early morning workers cross the square; outdoor exercises; kite-flying is a popular pastime; the top floors of the Radisson Hotel Shanghai New World, north of the square

Avenue), which divides the square in half. All places of interest, with the exception of the stand-out Shanghai Museum (▷ 42), are on the north side. Following the avenue east to west takes you past the Urban Planning Exhibition Center (▷ 37) to the Grand Theatre (▷ 45), north of which is the distinctive clock tower of the former Shanghai Art Museum, beyond which is the entrance to Renmin Park (▷ 40). Overlooking the square are some astronomically tall buildings, including Tomorrow Square, Brilliance Shimao International Plaza and the Radisson Hotel Shanghai New World (▷ 111). Unlike Beijing's Tiananmen Square, People's Square is not Stalinist in inspiration or sur-rounded by plain-clothes police. The square very much belongs to the people, who fill it with their own hobbies and pastimes, from ballroom danc-ing to pigeon-feeding and people-watching.

THE BASICS

🚇 G6
✉ People's Square
🍴 Restaurants and cafés
🚊 People's Square
🚌 46, 71, 123, 574
♿ Good

Renmin Park

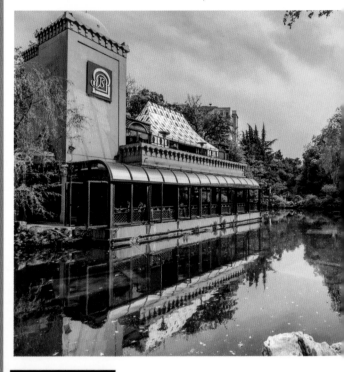

HIGHLIGHTS

● Museum of Contemporary Art
● People-watching
● Unhurried park tempo
● Lotus flowers in summer

TIP

● Greet the dawn in the park with enthusiasts who rise early for a tai chi lesson.

People's Park (Renmin Gongyuan) evolved from a former British racecourse. A much-needed enclave of greenery and tranquility, the park is an escape from the crowds of People's Square.

Park life Many visitors overlook the park, but it is lovely to have a stroll among its flower beds and manicured lawns. Be sure to visit the Museum of Contemporary Art (▷ 45), perhaps the chief attraction. Alongside the pond is Barbarossa (▷ 50), a popular Moroccan-style terrace bar and restaurant. The park attracts office workers at lunchtime and in summer any tree-shaded bench is much in demand. Summer is also the season to catch the gorgeous pink lotuses that flower in the waters of the main pond.

Gentle pursuits The racecourse had existed from 1862 and drew gamblers from around China, but it did not long survive the Communist takeover in 1949. Today, you'll see tai chi practitioners, stylized sword-fighters and kite flyers in the park's open spaces and on the adjoining People's Square (▷ 38). Groups of retired Chinese play mahjongg and chess, brush up on their ballroom dancing and English (native speakers out for a stroll are popular "victims" for the latter), and engage in match-making for their grandchildren, who are far too busy climbing the corporate ladder and having fun to find time for mere matrimony. Other parts of the park have narrow paths and fairly dense assemblages of trees and plants organized into a rigorously formal, landscaped setting.

THE BASICS

- ✚ G5–6
- ✉ Nanjing Xilu
- 🕐 Daily 6–6
- 🚇 People's Square
- 🚌 46, 71, 123, 574
- ✋ Free

Shanghai Museum

HIGHLIGHTS

● Paintings and ceramics
● Bronzes and sculpture
● Excellent presentation

TIP

● The audio tour is a very good investment, guiding you through the museum's many highlights.

The Shanghai Museum contains China's foremost collection of ceramics, bronzes, art, calligraphy and Buddhist statues. You'll need a whole day to do it justice, and you could easily find yourself coming back for more.

The museum The museum's exterior is an eye-catching design, with its square base and circular crown, from which emanate four archlike handles—the ensemble is supposed to represent a Han dynasty bronze mirror or an ancient bronze *ding* tripod (an ancient food vessel). Built in the very heart of the city in 1996 to house a collection of some 120,000 cultural relics, the museum has 11 galleries and three exhibition halls. Despite tough competition, it quite possibly still ranks as the nation's best museum.

Clockwise from left: The imposing entrance to the museum; Yi water vessel from 771BC; stone lions guarding the courtyard; Qing dynasty (17th–20th century) woman's embroidered velvet jacket; a wider view showing the circular upper level; a painting of a woman with a sword

Exhibits The thematic layout and good lighting display the exhibits to their best advantage. The principal galleries—which you really should not miss—are dedicated to ceramics, ancient bronzes, ancient Chinese sculpture and paintings. The ceramics section in particular is stunning—a majestic sweep from early pottery fragments to the gorgeous imperial pieces of the Ming and Qing dynasties. The dark patina bronzes are similarly spectacular, displaying the elaborate animistic patterns and designs of pre-Buddhist China. The ancient Chinese sculpture pieces are largely Buddhist in inspiration and subject, forming what is possibly the best collection in China. Other galleries are devoted to ancient Chinese jade, Ming and Qing furniture, art from China's ethnic minorities and Chinese calligraphy. Don't miss the excellent museum shop (▷ 49).

THE BASICS

www.shanghaimuseum.net
✚ G6
✉ 201 Renmin Dadao
☎ 6372 3500
🕐 Daily 9–5 (last entry 4pm)
🍴 Cafés on the premises
🚇 People's Square
♿ Good
💲 Free
❓ Audio tours (moderate for foreigners)

Xintiandi

TOP 25

Shikumen Open House Museum (left); a side street in the area (right)

THE BASICS

www.shanghaixintiandi.com

➕ G7

✉ Huangpi Nanlu

☎ 6311 2288

🍴 Many options

🚇 Huangpi Road (S)

🚌 42, 109 ♿ Good

ℹ Corner of Taicang Lu and Huangpi Nanlu

🕐 Daily 10–10

HIGHLIGHTS

● *Shikumen* (stone-frame) houses
● Taipingqiao Park
● Trendy restaurants and cafés
● Boutique stores

TIP

● Xintiandi is just the first part of a redevelopment project of the zone around Taipingqiao Park. It is interesting to peruse the district to see how the changes are progressing. Be sure to take time out for a stroll around the handsome park, which has a pond at its heart.

A heavily restored and rebuilt quadrant of *shikumen* architecture, Xintiandi is a stylish blend of trendy bars and cafés, celebrated restaurants, boutiques, galleries, museums and clubs.

Housing project Shanghai's distinctive *shikumen* housing developed in the 19th century, a fusion of Chinese courtyard architecture and British terrace housing. By the early 1900s styles had changed and the houses started falling into disrepair. In the 1990s developers hit on the idea of preserving the architecture of one run-down 1930s *shikumen* area by changing the buildings' function from residential to shops and restaurants—while preserving the exterior walls and tiles.

Private history The history of the area and the cultural significance of the buildings are explained in the superb Shikumen Open House Museum (north block, Xintiandi; daily 10.30–10.30), which also presents a picture of the daily life of a typical family living here in the 1930s. The rooms are crammed with everyday objects and personal effects—movie posters, typewriters, radios, scent bottles, toys. The *tingzijian*, or "staircase room," between the first and second floors was usually rented out because its north-facing aspect made it cold in winter and stiflingly hot in summer. The pithily named Memorial House of the First National Congress of the Communist Party of China speaks for itself. The main exhibit is a waxwork diorama dramatizing the founding congress of the Chinese Communist Party.

More to See

JING'AN SI (JING'AN TEMPLE)
www.shjas.org
The western part of Nanjing Lu was known as Bubbling Well Road until 1949. Before that it was Jing'an Road, named after this temple, which is over 1,700 years old. The original structures have mainly been rebuilt but restoration work is now complete.
➕ C5 ✉ 1686 Nanjing Xilu 🕐 Daily 7–5 🚇 Jing'an Temple 🚌 20, 37 ♿ None 💵 Inexpensive

SHANGHAI CENTRE
www.shanghaicentre.com
A colossal expat fixture on Nanjing Lu, the centre has shops, bars, restaurants, a supermarket, Starbucks, the Shanghai Centre Theatre (▷ 50) and the Portman Ritz-Carlton Shanghai hotel.
➕ D5 ✉ 1376 Nanjing Xilu ☎ 6279 8600 🚇 Jing'an Temple

SHANGHAI GRAND THEATRE
www.shgtheatre.com
China's first purpose-built opera house was designed by French architect Jean-Marie Charpentier

and opened in 1998. Performances include opera, classical music and musicals. The main stage is vast.
➕ G6 ✉ 300 Renmin Dadao ☎ 6386 8686 🚇 People's Square

SHANGHAI *LILONG* ARCHITECTURE
For some examples of Shanghai's *lilong* (alleyway) architecture, stroll west for around half a mile (around 1km) along Yuyuan Lu from the art deco Paramount Ballroom toward Zhenning Lu. On the way you'll pass some preserved 1930s *lilong* alleys with their characteristic houses.
➕ C5

SHANGHAI MUSEUM OF CONTEMPORARY ART (MOCA)
www.mocashanghai.org
A great addition to Shanghai's gallery selection, MOCA stages international exhibitions within a glass-walled and thoroughly modern exhibiting space.
➕ G6 ✉ Renmin Park ☎ 6327 9900 🕐 Daily 9–5 🚇 People's Square 💵 Inexpensive

The Shanghai Acrobatic Troupe performs at the Shanghai Centre Theatre

Jing'an Si occupies a site used for temples for the last 1,700 years

Nanjing Lu and People's Square

Nanjing Lu may no longer be the only shopping street in Shanghai, but it remains Shanghai's—and perhaps China's—most famous road.

DISTANCE: 2 miles (3km) **ALLOW:** 1.5 hours (not including stops)

START

PEACE HOTEL (▷ 62)
➕ J5 🚇 Nanjing Road (E)

1 Rising up alongside this first section of Nanjing Donglu, from the Peace Hotel, is the occasional art deco building and, of course, plenty of shops.

2 Walk westward from the Nanjing Road (E) Metro station at Henan Zhonglu along the street's most famous section, the pedestrians-only stretch to People's Square (but watch out for traffic there).

3 If you want to, jump on one of the small and inexpensive tourist "trains" that ferry passengers all the way along the pedestrianized length of Nanjing Donglu. You will pass numerous department stores, hotels and shops, including the Duoyunxuan Art Studio at No. 422 (▷ 48).

4 Pop into the Shanghai No. 1 Food Store (▷ 49), at No. 720, for every kind of Chinese snack.

END

PEOPLE'S SQUARE (▷ 38–39)
➕ G6 🚇 People's Square

7 Cross Renmin Dadao to the Shanghai Museum (▷ 42–43), the city's premier museum.

6 Exit the park and walk west, past the former Shanghai Art Museum building, or take the elevator to the foyer of the J.W. Marriott, high up in Tomorrow Square. Walk south to the Shanghai Grand Theatre (▷ 45), then east to the Urban Planning Exhibition Center (▷ 37).

5 Cross Xizang Zhonglu to Nanjing Xilu and turn south into Renmin Park to visit the Shanghai Museum of Contemporary Art (▷ 45).

Shopping

50 MOGANSHAN ROAD ART DISTRICT

www.m50.com.cn

Near Suzhou Creek, these art galleries, shops and cafés can easily take care of half a day. Look out for standout art galleries ShanghART (www.shangh artgallery.com) and Art Scene Warehouse (www.artscenewarehouse.com).

🚩 Off map ✉ 50 Moganshan Road ⏰ Hours vary, but most galleries open 10–6; some close Mon 🚇 Shanghai Railway Station

CITY PLAZA

www.jiu-guang.com

This high-end shopping center, also known as Jiu Guang, features top international brands including Tiffany, Armani, Estée Lauder and Barbour. It also has restaurants and a Japanese grocery store.

🚩 D5 ✉ 1618 Nanjing Xilu ☎ 3217 4838 ⏰ Daily 10–10 🚇 Jing'an Temple

CITY SHOP

www.cityshop.com.cn

Expats and visitors flock to the 11 branches of this supermarket for international delicatessen items, brand-name foods and more.

🚩 D5 ✉ Shanghai Centre, 1376 Nanjing Xilu ☎ 6279 8018 ⏰ Daily 8am–10pm 🚇 Jing'an Temple

DUOYUNXUAN ART STUDIO

www.duoyunxuan.com.cn

Come here for calligraphy, paintings, stationery, rubbings of ancient carvings and seals.

🚩 H5 ✉ 422 Nanjing Donglu ☎ 6360 6475 ⏰ Daily 9.30am–10pm 🚇 Nanjing Road (E)

ISETAN

www.isetan.cn/sh

Tokyo-based department store selling all the world's latest wares, though concentrating on items from Japan.

🚩 D5 ✉ 1376 Nanjing Xilu ☎ 6272 1111 ⏰ Daily 10am–9.30pm 🚇 Nanjing Road (E) 🚌 23, 112

LEI YUNG SHANG

www.leiyunshang.com

Traditional Chinese medicines may look quaint in the slick setting of Nanjing Lu, but this venerable practitioner has plenty of customers.

🚩 F5 ✉ 719 Nanjing Xilu ☎ 6217 9335 ⏰ Daily 8.30am–9pm 🚇 Nanjing Road (W)

NEW WORLD

www.newworldcoltd.com

From Adidas to Ermenegildo Zegna, by way of Cerruti 1881,

CLOISONNÉ

Bronze ornaments are covered in a network of copper strips and then filled with layers of enamel paint, before being fired and polished—this is cloisonné. Good pieces are hard to find, and the best tend to be found among the antiques.

Esprit, Lacoste, Swarovski and Versace, to name but a bare-bones few, the New World is nothing if not focused on known international brand names, and fits them all handily into its extensive floor space.

🚩 G5 ✉ 2–68 Nanjing Xilu ☎ 6358 8888 ⏰ Daily 10–10 🚇 People's Square

PLAZA 66

www.plaza66.com

Arguably the pick of the malls lining Shanghai's main shopping street, Plaza 66 is the place to head if money is no object. More than 100 designer brands are here, from Hermès to Bang & Olufsen.

🚩 E5 ✉ 1266 Nanjing Xilu ☎ 2225 1800 ⏰ Daily 10–10 🚇 Nanjing Road (W)

RAFFLES CITY

www.rafflescity.com.cn

This Singaporean-owned mall has won plaudits for being a well-designed and comfortable place to shop. It's especially good for casual clothes, with a good spread of popular chains. There's also a cinema and spa.

🚩 G6 ✉ 268 Xizang Zhonglu ☎ 6340 3600 ⏰ Daily 10–10 🚇 People's Square

SHANGHAI FASHION COMPANY

www.blszsd.com

Selling an extensive range of clothes at moderate prices, it is in part of a venerable building that once housed one of Shanghai's original department stores.

➕ H5 ✉ 650–690 Nanjing Donglu ☎ 6322 5445 ext123 🕑 Daily 9.30am–10pm 🚇 Nanjing Road (E)

SHANGHAI FOREIGN LANGUAGE BOOKSTORE

www.sbt.com.cn

This place has a decent selection of books in English and other languages, and books covering China, its culture and language. It also sells CDs and stationery.

➕ H6 ✉ 390 Fuzhou Lu ☎ 2320 4981 🕑 Daily 10–6.30 🚇 Nanjing Road (E) 🚌 17, 49

SHANGHAI JINGDEZHEN PORCELAIN ARTWARE STORE

Porcelain and handicrafts, many of them from the kilns at Jingdezhen, in Jiangxi province.

➕ E5 ✉ 1175 Nanjing Xilu ☎ 6253 0885 🕑 Daily 10–10 🚇 Nanjing Road (W) 🚌 20, 37

SHANGHAI MUSEUM SHOP

www.shanghaimuseum.net

In fact, there are three shops on the southern side of the museum, which specialize in books, antiques and antique reproductions.

➕ G6 ✉ 201 Renmin Dadao ☎ 6372 3500 🕑 Daily 9–5 🚇 People's Square 🚌 23

SHANGHAI NO. 1 FOOD STORE

This large supermarket stocks mainly Chinese products but has a growing range of international brands. It is a good resource for picnics or for when you don't want to eat out at a restaurant.

➕ H5 ✉ 720 Nanjing Donglu ☎ 6322 2777 🕑 Daily 9.30am–10pm 🚇 Nanjing Road (E) 🚌 20, 37

SHAO WAN SHENG

An institution in Shanghai, this shop was originally established as a grocery and snack store during the 1850s by a fisherman from Ningbo. Known as the "Snack King", its signature products are freshwater and seafood, such as spiral snails marinated in wine, dried herring and drunken hairy crabs.

➕ J5 ✉ 414 Nanjing Donglu ☎ 6322 4443 🕑 Daily 9am–10pm 🚇 Nanjing Road (E)

SPIN

Jingdezhen ceramics are irresistible with

their trendy, modern twist. The store is now in its new location after moving from the French Concession.

➕ D4 ✉ 360 Kangding Lu ☎ 6279 2545 🕑 Daily 10am–9pm 🚇 Changping Road

WESTGATE MALL

Another of the shopping malls that have sprouted along Nanjing Lu. Its stores feature haute couture and fashion boutiques among other trendy stores.

➕ E5 ✉ 1038 Nanjing Xilu ☎ 6218 7878 🕑 Daily 10–10 🚇 Nanjing Road (W)

YONG'AN

http://blyabh.blemall.com

This store was the renowned Wing On Department Store. It has now been reborn as an international-style shopping center.

➕ H5 ✉ 635 Nanjing Donglu ☎ 6322 4466 🚇 Nanjing Road (E) 🚌 20, 37

ZHANG XIAOQUAN KNIVES & SCISSORS STORE

www.shzhangxiaoquan.com

Famed as one of China's oldest stores, it has been in Shanghai for more than 100 years and in its present location for almost 60 years.

➕ H5 ✉ 490 Nanjing Donglu ☎ 6322 3858 🕑 Sun–Thu 9.30–9.30, Fri–Sat 9.30am–10pm 🚇 Nanjing Road (E)

Entertainment and Nightlife

BARBAROSSA

This Moroccan-themed bar, next to the pond in Renmin Park, is ideal for unwinding to great music.
➕ G5 ✉ Renmin Park, 231 Nanjing Xilu ☎ 6318 0220 🕐 Daily 11am–2am 🚇 People's Square

BIG BAMBOO

www.bigbamboo.asia
Perhaps the ultimate Shanghai sports bar, Big Bamboo is dedicated to beer, Western food, pool and back-to-back sports.
➕ D5 ✉ 132 Nanyang Lu ☎ 6256 2265 🕐 Daily 9.30am–1am 🚇 Jing'an Temple

FENNEL LOUNGE

Besides a small dining area, this venue has a cocktail bar plus a lounge with music—from DJs to live jazz and ethnic music.
➕ B6 ✉ 217 Zhenning Lu ☎ 3353 1773 🕐 Daily 11.30am–2am 🚇 Jiangsu Road

MAJESTIC THEATRE

One of Shanghai's finest old theaters, it is currently closed for renovations.
➕ E5 ✉ 66 Jiangning Lu 🚇 Nanjing Road (W)

MALONE'S BAR

www.malones.com.cn
This American-style bar offers bar food, live music and sports TV.
➕ D5 ✉ 255 Tongren Lu ☎ 6247 2400 🕐 Mon–Fri 11am–2am, Sat–Sun 12pm–2am 🚇 Jing'an Temple

MYST

http://mystshanghai.com
Three-story club opposite Jing'an Park with a huge middle-floor dance space, where events include parties with some of the world's top DJs. On the ground floor is a lounge bar, while the top floor is a VIP level.
➕ D6 ✉ 1123 Yan'an Zhong Lu ☎ 6437 9999 🕐 Daily 9.30pm til late 🚇 Jing'an Temple

SHANGHAI CENTRE THEATRE

www.shanghaicentre.com
One of the highlights of the Shanghai Centre (▷ 45), the theater hosts Chinese and international music, opera, drama and dance, along with performances by the Shanghai Acrobatic Theatre.
➕ D5 ✉ Shanghai Centre, 1376 Nanjing Xilu ☎ 6279 8948 🚇 Jing'an Temple

CHINESE OPERA

Chinese opera is unlike Western opera. Foreigners sometimes find it difficult to appreciate at first, but it is worth trying at least once. The singing style is falsetto and the action heavily stylized, but overall it is very colorful and can be highly dramatic, especially if battles are staged using acrobatic techniques. Check the local press for performances.

SHANGHAI CONCERT HALL

www.shanghaiconcerthall.org
Built as the Nanking Theatre in 1930, it was moved, brick by brick, to its present site in 2004. The 1,124-seat concert hall hosts many artists.
➕ G6 ✉ 523 Yan'an Donglu ☎ 6386 2836 🚇 People's Square 🚌 46, 71, 123, 454

SHANHAI GRAND THEATRE

See page 45.

SKY DOME BAR

www.radissonblu.com
Crowning the Radisson Hotel, this is one of the top places for truly astral views of Shanghai.
➕ G5 ✉ 47th floor, Radisson Hotel Shanghai New World, 88 Nanjing Xilu ☎ 6359 9999 🕐 Daily 5pm–1am 🚇 People's Square

STUDIO CITY

www.studiocitychina.com
A six-screen multiplex showing Chinese and international films, with some in English.
➕ E5 ✉ 10th Floor, Westgate Mall, 1038 Nanjing Xilu ☎ 6218 2173 🚇 Nanjing Road (W)

TIANCHAN YIFU THEATRE

www.tianchan.com
Head to this theater, which was renovated in 2004, for Chinese opera.
➕ G-H6 ✉ 701 Fuzhou Lu ☎ 6351 4668; reservations 6322 5294 🚇 People's Square 🚌 46, 71, 123, 574

PRICES

Prices are approximate, based on a 3-course meal for one person.
$$$ more than 250RMB
$$ 100–250RMB
$ under 100RMB

57° XIANG ($$)

If you like your food spicy, you will love this fiery Hunan version of Japanese teppanyaki.
➕ G7 ✉ 4th Floor, Infinity Plaza, 138 Huaihai Zhonglu ☎ 3315 0057 🕒 Daily 10–10 🚇 Dashijie

BELLA NAPOLI ($)

www.bellanapoli-sh.com
This good-value restaurant serves excellent pasta and other Italian dishes.
➕ E5 ✉ 73 Nanhui Lu ☎ 5289 0806 🕒 Daily 11–2, 5–11 🚇 Nanjing Road (W)

BRASIL STEAKHOUSE ($)

Waiters revolve around tables with hefty skewers of all-you-can-eat grilled meat—best for groups.
➕ C6 ✉ 1 Wanhangdu Lu ☎ 6255 9898 🕒 Daily 11–3, 5–11 🚇 Jing'an Temple

ELEMENT FRESH ($)

www.elementfresh.com
Sandwiches, salads and juices are offered at this popular café with several branches in Shanghai.
➕ D5 ✉ Room 112, Shanghai Centre, 1376 Nanjing Xilu ☎ 6279 8682 🕒 Daily 7am–11pm 🚇 Jing'an Temple

GONGDELIN ($–$$)

A famous vegetarian restaurant where the dishes are imitations of meat (using tofu).
➕ F6 ✉ 445 Nanjing Xilu ☎ 6327 0218 🕒 Daily lunch, dinner 🚇 People's Square 🚌 20

KATHLEEN'S 5 ($$–$$$)

www.kathleens5.com
On the fifth floor of the building that was formerly the Shanghai Art Museum (and with a glassed-in rooftop terrace), this smart restaurant serves American-based cuisine that roams the world for elements to mix and match, with local influences. Brunch is served from 11am on weekends.
➕ G6 ✉ 325 Nanjing Xilu ☎ 6327 2221 🕒 Mon–Thu 11.30am–midnight, Fri 11.30am–1am, Sat, Sun 11am–1am 🚇 People's Square 🚌 46, 71, 123, 574

LYNN ($–$$)

Excellent, modern and eye-catching Shanghai

SOUP

In the West it is customary to have soup as a starter or appetizer, but in China soup is generally served toward the end of the meal as a sort of "digestif," and on informal occasions is also a way of helping to finish remains in the rice bowl. At formal functions such as banquets, soup is served in a separate bowl.

cuisine in a sharp and stylish environment. Try the crispy duck or the deep-fried spare ribs.
➕ D5 ✉ 99-1 Xikang Lu ☎ 6247 0101 🕒 Daily 11.30–2, 5–10.15 🚇 Nanjing Road (W)

MEI LONG ZHEN ($$)

In the former Communist Party headquarters, this restaurant serves food in Huaiyang, Sichuan and Shanghainese styles. Deep-fried *gui* (fish), tofu dishes and cold shredded jellyfish are on the menu.
➕ G6 ✉ 1081 Nanjing Xilu ☎ 6253 5353 🕒 Daily lunch, dinner 🚇 Nanjing Road (W) 🚌 37

T8 ($$–$$$)

www.t8-shanghai.com
At the heart of Xintiandi, elegant T8 is one of Shanghai's very best restaurants for international dishes and pure ambience. Treat yourself.
➕ G7 ✉ No. 8, North Block, Xintiandi, Lane 181 Taicang Lu ☎ 6355 8999 🕒 Daily 11.30–2.30, 6.30–11.30 🚇 Huangpi Road (S)

VEGETARIAN LIFESTYLE ($–$$)

www.jujubetree.com
Excellent meat-free, organic and MSG-devoid Chinese food—all tasty and imaginatively created. The restaurant has two other branches.
➕ E5 ✉ 258 Fengxian Lu ☎ 6215 7566 🕒 Daily 11.30–9.30 🚇 Nanjing Road (W)

Stretching north from Renmin Lu on the edge of the Old City to Suzhou Creek, the Bund is Shanghai's premier promenade. From here you have a stunning view across the water to Pudong's glittering towers.

WUSONG LU

Hanyang Lu

Tanggu Lu

Hongkou Lu

Minhang Lu

Xi'an Lu

Nankun Lu

Liyang Lu

Hongkou Lu

International
Cruise Terminal

Dongchangzhi Lu

Lu

Dongchangzhi

Machang Lu

Tangu Lu

Branch

Shangqiu Lu

Yongding Lu

DONGDAMING LU

DAMING LU

Astor
House
Hotel

Minhang Lu

Lingxun

International
Passenger
Terminal

Huangpu Lu

Huangpu

XINJIAN LU TUNNEL

K

L

Around Suzhou Creek

HIGHLIGHTS

- Waibaidu Bridge
- Former British Consulate
- Russian Consulate
- Astor House Hotel
- Broadway Mansions
- Shanghai Post Museum

TIP

- It is more pleasant these days to stroll the riverside paths along either bank. The occasional sorry-looking green scraps of yore have been joined by riverside parks, gardens and walkways, with more to follow in the years to come.

Long a feature of the Shanghai land-scape, Suzhou Creek came to represent much that was unattractive in Shanghai's rush to develop. Today, it's a sign of how the city is cleaning up its act.

The colonial period Suzhou Creek separated the British and American Concession, and the creek banks close to the Huangpu River have some architectural survivors from this time. The Broadway Mansions Hotel, at 20 Suzhou Beilu, is in an art deco masterpiece that was the Shanghai Mansions (1934). Also on the north bank, the Astor House Hotel (▷ 63), at 15 Huangpu Lu, is a historic survivor from concession days, as is the Russian Consulate opposite. The twin-span steel Waibaidu (Garden) Bridge, which crosses over the creek alongside Huangpu Park (▷ 63), dates from 1907,

Clockwise from left: Vessels line the sides of the creek and traffic passes along the middle; selling bicycle registrations near Suzhou Bridge; the Russian Consulate building; a new apartment block on the creekside; Suzhou Creek artists' quarter

replacing a wooden bridge; it was taken away for restoration in 2008 and put back in 2009. The old Shanghai Post Office building, at 276 Suzhou Beilu, houses the intriguing Shanghai Post Museum.

Troubled waters From its source in Tai Hu (Lake Tai) close to Suzhou, the creek flows east through some of China's most polluted territory before debouching into the Huangpu River at the north end of the Bund. By 1998, when the first clean-up measures were introduced, Suzhou Creek's once crystal-clear water had become a black open sewer. Those who lived beside the creek—a fate reserved for the poor—could not open their windows in summer so bad was the smell. The Suzhou Creek Rehabilitation Project has changed things for the better. More needs to be done, but fish are returning.

THE BASICS

⊞ H5–K5
✉ Suzhou Nanlu and Suzhou Beilu
🚇 Nanjing Road (E)
🚌 20, 55, 65

The Bund

HIGHLIGHTS

● Panoramic views
● Waterfront European-style buildings
● Boat trips on the Huangpu River (▷ 60)

TIP

● The Bund shows different faces of itself during the day: Early morning tai chi practitioners give way to rush-hour crowds, then a period of calm before the lunchtime and afternoon strollers emerge. Evening, the time for leisure crowds, is followed by those out to view the lights.

Arriving by ship from Europe or America in the 1930s, the expatriate's first view of Shanghai would have been the waterfront street known as the Bund, a grand slice of the colonial world that is still impressive today.

Waitan The Bund (meaning "waterfront" or "embankment") is now known as Waitan or Zhongshan Dong Yilu (or 1-Lu). It runs along the Huangpu River from Suzhou Creek in the north to Yan'an Lu in the south. The buildings lining it date from the early 20th century and are largely Western in style. The Bund is where modern Shanghai began and it remains the city's grandest display. A "must do" activity is to stroll the Bund after dark, when the illuminated waterfront and the view to Pudong create a memorable vista.

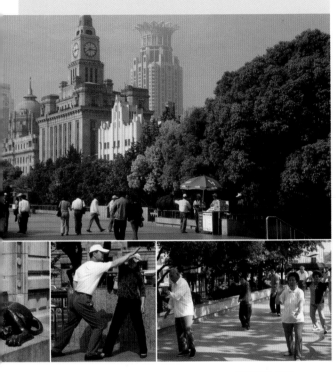

Clockwise from left: A flag flying atop the Customs House clock tower; statue of Chen Yi, the first mayor of Shanghai; the Bund viewed from the Riverside Promenade; tai chi exercises; a bronze lion outside the Hong Kong and Shanghai Bank

The buildings Although changes have been made—the trams have gone, as have the old "go-downs," or warehouses, and statues of foreigners—the Bund would be recognizable to a 1930s resident. A walk from south to north would begin with the Shanghai Club at No. 3, which claimed to have the longest bar in the world. The domed building at No. 12 was the Hong Kong and Shanghai Bank, built in 1923; it is definitely worth popping in to look at the ceiling mosaics inside. Next door, surmounted by a clock once known as Big Ching, is the Customs House of 1927. Next to the main building of the Peace Hotel (▷ 62) on the corner of Nanjing Lu (Nanking Road) is the Bank of China (1937). No. 27 was the head-quarters of Jardine Matheson, one of the early companies to prosper from the opium trade, and No. 33 was the old British Consulate.

THE BASICS

✚ J6–K5
✉ Zhongshan Dong 1-Lu
🍴 Various restaurants and cafés
🚇 Nanjing Road (E)
♿ Few

Huangpu Riverboat Tour

- Fabulous panoramas of both the Bund and Lujiazui in Pudong
- Confluence with the mighty Yangtze River
- Yangpu Bridge

TIP

- Should a cruise on the Huangpu take up more time or money than you can afford, try instead the cross-river ferries, which you can think of as giving a cheap microcruise on the river.

The Huangpu and Yangtze rivers are the original reasons for Shanghai's prosperity. A river cruise along the Huangpu will show aspects of this huge city you might not otherwise see.

Two rivers The Yangtze is the longest river in China. Rising in the Tibetan Plateau, it meanders across the country, passing through several provinces, and, most famously, the Three Gorges. The Huangpu, only 68 miles (110km) in length, runs from Dianshan Lake and empties into the Yangtze River some 17 miles (28km) downstream. Its average width through the city is 1,300ft (400m) and its average depth 26ft (8m). Large ships were able to enter the wide mouth of the Yangtze, make the short journey up the Huangpu and unload their cargoes at the wharves along

Clockwise from left: A plaque showing the level of the Huangpu flood in 1997; a cloudy night at the Bund; crowds on the Bund looking across to Pudong

the Bund. The goods were transported by barges along Suzhou Creek and then along the network of canals for distribution throughout China.

Touring the Huangpu Boat tours leave from Shiliupu Wharf in Old Town, south of the intersection between Remin Lu and Zhongshan Dong 1-Lu. The shortest trips merely journey past the International Cruise Passenger Terminal and back, while the longest trip is the three-and-a-half-hour return journey to Wusongkou at the mouth of the Yangtze River. If you travel first class, the trip to Wusongkou and back is comfortable. You first pass Suzhou Creek, then the new Shanghai Port International Ferry Terminal and Yangpu Bridge. You will also pass Fuxing Island, where Chiang Kai Shek made his last stand before fleeing to Taiwan. Finally, you meet the Yangtze, before returning.

THE BASICS

➕ L5

✉ Boats leave from Shiliupu Wharf in Old Town, close to Yuyuan on Zhongshan Dong 1-Lu (➕ K7)

☎ 6374 4461

🕐 Cruises depart daily every 2 hours or so 9am–10pm

🍴 Bar on board ship

🚌 55, 65

♿ Good

💰 Expensive—tickets through CITS or from a kiosk close to the pier

❓ Performances often given on river cruise

Peace Hotel

The Peace Hotel alongside the Bank of China (left); the hotel's Old Jazz Band (right)

THE BASICS

www.fairmont.com/peace-hotel-shanghai
+ J5
⊠ 20 Nanjing Donglu
☎ 6321 6888
◉ All year
🍴 Café, bars and restaurants on premises
🚇 Nanjing Road (E)
🚌 37, 42, 55, 65
♿ Good
💷 Free, unless you spend the night

HIGHLIGHTS

● Art deco architecture
● Art deco details in the lobby

The Peace Hotel is the most iconic art deco building in Shanghai. During its heyday, this was *the* place to stay and the patina of its pyramid roof is one of the Bund's most distinctive images.

The Sassoons Of the many families of Sephardic Jews, the most famous is the Sassoon family. Fleeing an intolerant Baghdad in the 18th century to make a fortune in Bombay, they then proceeded to buy warehouses in Shanghai. Successive generations invested in the port, but it was Victor Sassoon who built the well-known landmark on the Bund now known as the Peace Hotel. Though it represents the hated era of foreign domination, many new skyscrapers ape its distinctive pyramidical roof design.

The Cathay There had been a Sassoon House on the Bund for some time, but Victor Sassoon had visions of a skyscraper as a business headquarters and wanted to include a hotel into the bargain. Today's Peace Hotel, originally the Cathay, dates from 1930, with art deco ironwork and high ceilings inside and looking somewhat like a smaller Empire State Building outside. The lowest four floors were reserved for offices; the remainder were given over to what Victor hoped would be the finest hotel in the East. It had the best technology and service that the period could offer, while the Horse & Hounds Bar became the most fashionable rendezvous in the city. Renovated and reopened as the Fairmont Peace Hotel, it once again attracts the in-crowd.

More to See

ASTOR HOUSE HOTEL

www.astorhousehotel.com

Now restored as a fancy hotel (▷ 110), this building just across the bridge at the Bund's northern end was once one of the city's finest hotels.

🞧 K5 ✉ 15 Huangpu Lu ☎ 6324 6388 🕐 Daily 🚇 Nanjing Road (E) 🚌 28 ⛑ Good 🎫 Free

BUND SIGHTSEEING TUNNEL

This psychedelically lit tunnel runs from the Bund, opposite Nanjing Donglu, to the Pudong shore. You board an unmanned miniature train car for the four-minute ride, during which a sound-and-light show unfolds.

🞧 J6–K6 ✉ Zhongshan Dong 1-Lu (the Bund) 🕐 Mon–Thu 8am–10.30pm, Fri–Sun 8am–11pm (to 10pm daily Nov–Mar) 🚇 Nanjing Road (E) 🚌 65 🎫 Moderate

HUANGPU PARK

At the northern end of the Bund near the bridge, this is the infamous park where a notice was said to forbid entry to "Dogs and Chinese" (the wording was not exactly like that, in fact). It is a pleasant park with an ugly monument, beneath which is a small museum about old Shanghai.

🞧 K5 ✉ Zhongshan Dong 1-Lu (the Bund) 🕐 Summer daily 6am–10pm; winter 6–6 🚇 Nanjing Road (E) ⛑ None 🎫 Free

ROCKBUND ART MUSEUM (RAM)

www.rockbundartmuseum.org

Acclaimed contemporary art gallery in the former Royal Asiatic Society building, it offers contemporary photography and art.

🞧 J5 ✉ 120 Huqiu Lu ☎ 3310 9985 🕐 Tue–Sat 10–6 🎫 Moderate 🚇 Nanjing Road (E)

SHANGHAI GALLERY OF ART

www.threeonthebund.com

This exclusive gallery, in the prestigious Three on the Bund shopping, dining and entertainment complex, displays contemporary art.

🞧 J6 ✉ 3rd floor, Three on the Bund, Zhongshan Dong 1-Lu ☎ 6321 5757 🕐 See website for exhibition dates 🎫 Free 🚇 Nanjing Road (E)

Early morning exercises in Huangpu Park

A street artist in Huangpu Park

The Bund

The very symbol of 19th-century foreign interventions in China, the Bund (▷ 58–59) was where the story of modern Shanghai began.

DISTANCE: 1.2 miles (2km) **ALLOW:** Up to 1 hour

START

SUZHOU CREEK (▷ 56)
🚇 K5 🚉 Nanjing Road (E)

1 From Waibaidu Bridge at Suzhou Creek, walk south down the west side of Zhongshan Dong 1-Lu. One of the first buildings you will see is the former British Consulate, behind the gates at No. 33.

2 The House of Roosevelt, at 1920s Beaux-Arts icon No. 27, boasts a climate-controlled wine cellar.

3 The Peace Hotel (▷ 62) stands on the corner of Nanjing Donglu. Over the road is a second wing of the Peace Hotel, once the Palace Hotel and now the Swatch Art Peace Hotel.

4 Continue south, crossing Jiujiang Lu, Hankou Lu and Fuzhou Lu, taking in details on buildings like the Customs House at No. 13 and the former Hong Kong and Shanghai Bank at No. 12.

END

ASTOR HOUSE HOTEL (▷ 63)
🚇 K5 🚉 Nanjing Road (E)

7 At the north end of the Bund, stroll through Huangpu Park (▷ 63), then cross Waibaidu Bridge to visit the venerable Astor House Hotel on the north side of Suzhou Creek.

6 Cross over Zhongshan Dong 1-Lu, and go north along the Bund's waterfront promenade, affording you a different view of the buildings you have just passed, and views to Pudong's skyscrapers.

5 On the south side of Guangdong Lu, at No. 3, is the stellar Three on the Bund shopping, dining and cultural complex.

THE BUND/WAITAN WALK

Shopping

BLUE SHANGHAI WHITE
www.blueshanghaiwhite.com
Perfect hand-painted ceramic gifts.
➕ J6 ✉ Room 103, 17 Fuzhou Lu ☎ 6323 0856 🕐 Daily 10.30–6.30 🚇 Nanjing Road (E)

LAO ZHOU HU CHENG CHINESE WRITING BRUSH AND INKSTICK STORE
www.laozhouhuchen.com
This shop supplies the items needed for traditional Chinese painting and calligraphy—brushes, inkstones and ink slabs, for example.
➕ J5 ✉ 280 Fuzhou Lu ☎ 5169 8918 🕐 Daily 9–5.30 🚇 Nanjing Road (E) 🚌 66

SILK KING
www.silkking.com
One of Shanghai's most popular silk outlets for silk by the meter or tailor-made clothes.
➕ J5 ✉ 588 Nanjing Donglu ☎ 6321 2193 🚇 Nanjing Road (E)

SUZHOU COBBLERS
www.suzhou-cobblers.com
Choose from a wide range of exquisite hand-embroidered Chinese silk slippers, or pick one of the handbags that come in a variety of colors and designs, for a reminder of your time in Shanghai.
➕ J6 ✉ Room 101, 17 Fuzhou Lu ☎ 6321 7087 🕐 Daily 10–6.30 🚇 Nanjing Road (E)

Entertainment and Nightlife

BAR ROUGE
www.bar-rouge-shanghai.com
The coolest cocktail bar in town, the atmosphere is ramped up by DJs after midnight.
➕ J6 ✉ 18 Zhongshan Dong 1-Lu (the Bund) ☎ 6339 1199 🕐 Mon–Thu 3pm–2am, Fri, Sat 3pm–4am; special brunch Sat–Sun noon–4pm 🚇 Nanjing Road (E) 🚌 37, 42, 55, 65

CAPTAIN'S BAR
Atop the Captain Hostel (▷ 109), this lively and inexpensive bar has an excellent terrace with views of Lujiazui.
➕ J6 ✉ 6th floor, Captain Hostel, 37 Fuzhou Lu ☎ 6323 7869 🕐 Daily 5pm–10pm 🚇 Nanjing Road (E)

GLAMOUR BAR
www.m-restaurantgroup.com
A gorgeous bar offering fabulous cocktails, vibrant views and a stylish ambience.
➕ J6 ✉ 6th Floor, 20 Guangdong Lu ☎ 6350 9988 🕐 Daily 5pm–2 or 3am 🚇 Nanjing Road (E) 🚌 37, 42, 55, 65

M18
www.bund18.com
Billing itself as the "Sexiest Boutique Nightclub" in Shanghai, this sophisticated nightspot features a luminous bar and top DJs.
➕ J6 ✉ 4th floor, Bund 18, 18 Zhongshan Dong 1-Lu (the Bund) ☎ 6339 1200 🕐 Tue–Sat 8pm–2am (lounge), Tue–Sat 9pm–2am (club) 🚇 Nanjing Road (E)

SIR ELLY'S TERRACE
http://shanghai.peninsula.com
Offering views across the Huangpu River, this U-shaped rooftop bar atop the Peninsula Shanghai has the Bund's largest terrace and throngs with Shanghai's elite.
➕ J5 ✉ 14th floor, 32 Zhongshan Dong 1-Lu (the Bund) ☎ 6373 3588 🕐 Sun–Thu 5pm–midnight, Fri–Sat 5pm–1am 🚇 Nanjing Road (E)

Restaurants

PRICES

Prices are approximate, based on a 3-course meal for one person.
$$$ more than 250RMB
$$ 100–250RMB
$ under 100RMB

AJISEN ($)

www.ajisen.com.cn
Ajisen's Japanese noodles have developed a loyal following across the entire land. Service is efficient, although you may have to wait for a table. The photo menu makes choosing your food easy; you pay at the start of the meal.
➕ J5 ✉ 479 Nanjing Donglu ☎ 6360 7194 🕐 Daily 10–10 Ⓜ Nanjing Road (E)

THE BUND BREWERY ($–$$)

www.thebundbrewery.com.cn
A brewpub that introduced the first micro-brewed German beer to Shanghai 20 years ago, it also serves up Chinese and Western food.
➕ J6 ✉ 11 Hankou Lu ☎ 6321 8447 🕐 Daily 11am–1am Ⓜ Nanjing Road (E) 🚌 49

GRAND BRASSERIE ($$$)

www.waldorfastoriashanghai.com
One of three restaurants at the sophisticated and opulent Waldorf Astoria hotel, it offers chic but casual all-day dining with an East-meets-West menu. Its Champagne Brunch on Sundays is to die for.

➕ J6 ✉ 2 Zhongshan Dong 1-Lu (the Bund) ☎ 6322 9988 🕐 Daily 6–10.30, 11.30–3, 5.30–11 Ⓜ Nanjing Road (E) 🚌 37, 42, 55, 65

JEAN GEORGES ($$–$$$)

www.jean-georges.com
Offering stupendous dishes in a lavish setting, this is one of Shanghai's best restaurants for modern Western cuisine.
➕ J6 ✉ 4th floor, Three on the Bund, 3 Zhongshan 1-Lu ☎ 6321 7733 🕐 Daily 11.30–2.30, 6–11 (Sat–Sun 11.30–3) Ⓜ Nanjing Road (E)

M ON THE BUND ($$)

www.m-restaurantgroup.com
M on the Bund serves European dishes and is one of Shanghai's best restaurants, especially if you can grab a terrace table with its wonderful views. Reserve ahead.
➕ J6 ✉ 7th floor, 20 Guangdong Lu ☎ 6350 9988 🕐 Mon–Fri 11.30–2.30, 6–10.30, Sat–Sun 11.30–3, 3–5 Ⓜ Nanjing Road (E)

DUMPLINGS

Like north China's famous *jiaozi* (dumplings), Shanghai's signature dish—copied across the nation—is *xiaolongbao* (pronounced "seeyaolong-bough"). Small, steamed, plump dumplings, *xiaolong-bao* come in a variety of fillings, from pork to crab meat, arriving at the table in steamers. Bite carefully, as the meat juice is scalding.

MR & MRS BUND ($–$$)

www.bund18.com
www.mmbund.com
French food with a fusion twist and views across to Pudong from this uber-cool restaurant on the 6th floor of the Bund 18 building. Arrive early or make a reservation to get a window table.
➕ J6 ✉ 6th floor, 18 Zhongshan Dong 1-Lu (the Bund) ☎ 6323 9898 🕐 Daily 5.30–10.30pm (also Thu–Sat 11pm–2am) Ⓜ Nanjing Road (E) 🚌 37, 42, 55, 65

NEW HEIGHTS ($)

Put yourself up there with the best: It's a tall order not to be won over by the Shanghai views at night at this bar-cum-restaurant, serving international cuisine.
➕ J6 ✉ 7th floor, Three on the Bund, 3 Zhongshan Dong 1-Lu ☎ 6321 0909 🕐 Daily noon–10.30pm Ⓜ Nanjing Road (E)

WHAMPOA CLUB ($$$)

Run by celebrity chef, Jereme Leung, this smart restaurant, on the fifth floor of the Three on the Bund center, offers a contemporary, fusion take on Shanghai cuisine.
➕ J6 ✉ Three on the Bund, 3 Zhongshan Dong 1-Lu (entrance at 17 Guangdong Lu) ☎ 6321 3737 🕐 Daily 11.30–2.30, 5.30–11 Ⓜ Nanjing Road (E) 🚌 37, 42, 55, 65

The rickety Old Town contains the Yu Garden, the Yuyuan Bazaar, Huxinting Tea House, several notable temples and antiques markets, and an escape from Shanghai's more frantic districts.

5

6

7

8

9

Jinling

Donglu

Nanlu

Sichuan

Yong'an

ZHONGSHAN

Xinyong'an Lu

RENMIN

LU

Yuyuan
Garden

Fuyou

Lu

Changsheng

Chenxiangge
Nunnery

Chenxiangge Lu

Anren

Fuyou

Gucher
Park

**Bai Yun Guan
(White Cloud Temple)**

Qinglian

Nanlu

Henan

**Yuyuan
(Yu Garden)**

**Dajing
Pavilion**

Dajing

Zihua Lu

**Yuyuan
Bazaar**

**Chenghuang Mia
(Temple of the
City God)**

RENMIN

Wanzhu Jie

Luxiangyuan

Shizi Jie

Malle

**Fuyou
Market**

Fangbang

Zhonglu

**Huxinting
Tea House**

Zhonglu

Jie

Beishih Long

Shipi Long

Xuelongai

Zhoulin

Fang

Songxue

Yaola an
Long

Zhongfu

Qiujia

Jie

Sanbaolu

Jie

Xueyuan

Jukur

Long

Jinli

Kongjia

Long

Dongliu

**Xiaotaoyuan
Mosque**

Tongzi

Long

Jie

Dongliu

Xivaolle

Long

Fuxing

Jingxiu lu

Xicangqiao

Long

Fuxing

Yichuan

Spandl

Fuxing

LAO XI MEN

Menghua

**Wen Miao
(Confucian
Temple)**

Zhuhua
Jie

Wenmiao

Nanlu

Wangon

Xitangia Jie

Meijia

Dongliu

Anian Lu

ZHONGHUA

Penglai

Xiaolan

Ynxao

lu

Henan

**NANSHI
(OLD TOWN)**

Qiaojia

Dali Lu

Qiaojia

Yuilan

Yundao

ZHONGHUA

Dalin

Dalin

Daxing

shangwen

Jie

Huangja
Jie

Ningme

Yuila
Long

Guangqi

Xiaonanmen

Wanglamatou

Saja

Meru

Jie

LUJIABANG

YINGXUN

LU

Wiebang

Houjie

Dachang Jie

Jiangyin

Puyu

Xiao

Long

Kuolong

Dongdiangyin

Jie

Dongjiangyin

Long

DONGJIADU

Xiaotuyi

Long

LU

0   400 m

0   400 yds

G

H

J

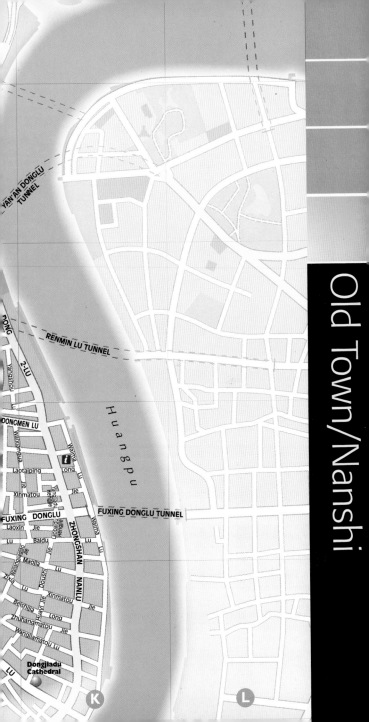

YAN'AN DONGLU TUNNEL

DONG

2-LU

Yangshou

RENMIN LU TUNNEL

DONGMEN LU

Waixiangua

Laotaiping

Xinmatou

Jie

Long

H u a n g p u

Waima

FUXING DONGLU

Laoxin

Jie

Lu

Baidu

ZHONGSHAN

Maolia

NANLU

Waima

FUXING DONGLU TUNNEL

Lu

Zixa

Xinmatou

Beishijia

Jie

Long

Zhuhangmatou

Lu

Wangjamatou Lu

Dongjiadu Cathedral

LU

K

L

Huxinting Tea House

TOP
25

HIGHLIGHTS

● Charming building in entertaining location
● Cooling on hot days

TIP

● When the waiter or waitress refills your tea cup, tapping the index and second fingers of your right hand is a traditional way to indicate "thank you" for being served tea—the gesture represents the kowtow that everyone had to do in the presence of the emperor.

The delightful old teahouse, in its watery setting in the middle of a lake, is the focal point of the Old Town. It fits in with the China of popular imagination, a China that has all but disappeared.

Tea drinking Tea is widely produced throughout central and southern China and is also widely consumed in everyday life—taxi drivers often keep a jar with them, half filled with leaves to which boiling water is added throughout the day; there will probably be tea in your hotel room; and when people meet, or at an official function, tea will certainly be served at some point. In the past, every town had several teahouses, where conversation was an adjunct to an appreciation of good teas. However, an appreciation of fine teas and the art of tea drinking in its ceremonial form,

Clockwise from top left: A suited waiter in the tea house; people negotiating the Nine Zig-Zag Bridge to the teahouse; visitors to Shanghai enjoying tea; the teahouse illuminated at night; relaxing with tea and snacks

where such matters as the quality of the water used are much considered, has largely vanished.

Huxinting The Huxinting Tea House, surrounded by a small lake, is truly the hub of the Old Town. Its precise origins are not entirely clear, but it dates from some time during the Ming dynasty, was renovated as a brokerage house in 1784, and became a teahouse in 1856. It was originally part of both the Temple of the City God (▷ 75) and Yuyuan (▷ 74). As Shanghai prospered, parts of the garden, including the teahouse, were purchased by local merchants, who used it as a meeting place for conducting business. A building of great charm, it is approached via the Nine Zig-Zag Bridge, over waters glittering with goldfish. Inside you may drink good-quality tea from traditional teapots—refreshing on hot summer days.

THE BASICS

www.yuyuantm.com.cn

✚ J7

✉ 257 Yuyuan Lu

☎ 6373 6950

🕓 Mon–Fri 8.30am–9.30pm, Sat–Sun 8am–10pm

🍴 Plenty of restaurants nearby, in the Old Town

Ⓜ Yuyuan Garden

🚌 14, 26

♿ None

💰 Moderate

❓ Tea ceremony performed in the evening

Old Town

HIGHLIGHTS

● A hint of the atmosphere of old China
● Excellent snack food and shops

TIP

● Most visitors to the Old Town focus on its northern section, around Yuyuan and the Huxinting Tea House. But there's much more to the district than this, and, if anything, the other parts are more authentic.

One of the unexpected pleasures of Shanghai is to discover, amid the high-rise modernity, an old Chinese town—the original Shanghai. In its narrow streets you can absorb something of the atmosphere and bustle of traditional China.

History Until the Treaty of Nanking in 1842, Shanghai was a moderately important walled town concentrated in the area now called Nanshi. The walls were pulled down in 1912 to provide better access for shops and traders, but even now the area is self-contained and the route of the old walls can be traced along Renmin Lu and Zhonghua Lu. A single chunk of wall survives at the Dajing Pavilion (▷ 75). Some of Shanghai's most ancient temples survive in the Old Town, including the Wen Miao (Confucius Temple;

Clockwise from top left: Collectibles at Dongtai Lu antiques market; an Old Town tailor hard at work on her sewing machine; renovated stores; the Bird and Flower Market; a small tailoring shop; steamed dumplings ready for sale; Bai Yun Guan (White Cloud Temple)

▷ 76), the Chenghuang Miao (▷ 75) and the Chenxiangge Nunnery (▷ 75). The signature sight is the Yuyuan (▷ 74) and the surrounding bazaar.

Today The Old Town has been spared much of the over-development that has robbed Shanghai of so much history. Although some rebuilding has taken place, the old Chinese town retains its pre-war atmosphere, stuffed with narrow lanes above which washing is hung out to dry. The disheveled streets are filled with I specialist shops selling walking sticks or tea, and markets overflowing with food, collectibles and knickknacks. There are several antiques markets, but you'll need a discerning eye to select genuine items. The Yuyuan Bazaar (▷ 76) brims with shops selling traditional gift items. A variety of teahouses and restaurants are also at hand for recuperation after sightseeing.

THE BASICS

✚ H7–J9
🍽 Plenty of restaurants in the area
🚇 Yuyuan Garden
♿ None
🎟 Free

Yuyuan

TOP 25

A willow overhangs a pond in the garden (left); detail of a building (right)

THE BASICS

www.yugarden.com.cn

🚇 J7

✉ 218 Anren Jie, Old Town

🕑 Daily summer 8.30–5.30, winter 8.30–5 (last entry 30 minutes before closing time)

🍴 Plenty of restaurants nearby, in the Old Town

🚇 Yuyuan Garden

🚌 26

💷 Moderate

HIGHLIGHTS

● Rockeries, bridges and pavilions
● Miniature fish-filled lake and pavilion

TIP

● Yuyuan can be crowded, particularly on summer weekends. Try to visit early in the morning or at lunchtime.

Shanghai does have its surprises. Hidden from casual observation in the heart of the Old Town is one of the finest surviving classical gardens in China.

The Pan family The Yuyuan, or Yu Garden, has a long history. It was created in the mid-16th century by Pan Yunduan as an act of filial affection for his father. Pan, a native of Shanghai who had been in public service in Sichuan Province, must have been a wealthy and influential figure, for the garden takes up almost 5ha (12 acres), a large chunk of the Old Town. By the time it was completed in 1587, however, Pan's father had died, and although additions were made to the garden from time to time, it suffered from neglect. Twice in the 19th century it was used as headquarters—in 1842 by the British Land Force and in the 1850s by the Small Swords Society, dedicated to the restoration of the Ming dynasty.

Today's garden The Yu Garden exemplifies the classic Ming garden, where rock gardens, bridges and ponds surround pavilions and corridors to create an illusion of a natural landscape. In reality, although the materials used are the work of nature, the design is very obviously the work of man. But what is important in this garden is the "harmony of scale," its beauty lying in the intricate design, which in the past would have permitted tranquil contemplation in a comparatively small area. An unusual feature is the sculpted dragon that curls around the top of the garden wall.

More to See

BAI YUN GUAN (WHITE CLOUD TEMPLE)

Relocated quite a few years ago from its former location to the west of the Old Town, this Taoist temple is quite modern in feel but is worth a look to compare and contrast with Buddhist temples.

➕ H7 ✉ 239 Dajing Lu 🕐 Daily 8–4.30 🚇 Dashijie 🖐 Inexpensive

CHENGHUANG MIAO (TEMPLE OF THE CITY GOD)

The Temple of the City God has been reconstructed more than 20 times since it was founded in 1403, but its popularity with devotees, especially those praying for wealth and prosperity, remains undiminished. The hall of the City God is to the rear of the building, beyond the inner courtyard, where you may see red-robed trainee monks, a reminder that this is very much a working temple.

➕ J7 ✉ 249 Fangbang Zhonglu (at Yu Garden) 🕐 Daily 8.30–4.30 🚇 Yuyuan Garden 🚫 None 🖐 Inexpensive

CHENXIANGGE NUNNERY

This small Buddhist temple belonged to the Pan family, who built Yuyuan. It takes its name from an eaglewood statue of the Buddha, which gives off a resinous scent in damp weather.

➕ J7 ✉ 2a Chenxiangge Lu 🕐 Daily 7–4 🚇 Yuyuan Garden ✉ 11, 24, 26 🚫 None 🖐 Inexpensive

DAJING PAVILION

The Old Town Wall was felled at the end of the Qing dynasty and this is the last remnant. The small preserved section of battlements can be climbed, but it's more interesting as a monument to a vanished era.

➕ H7 ✉ Dajing Lu 🕐 Daily 9–5 🚇 Dashijie 🖐 Inexpensive

DONGJIADU CATHEDRAL

www.sfx.sh

Built by Spanish Jesuits in 1853 as the St. Xavier cathedral, in a style reminiscent of Iberian colonial baroque, Dongjiadu is the oldest Catholic church in Shanghai and stands outside the southeastern edge of

Statue of Confucius at Wen Miao temple (▷ 76)

Worshipers at Chenxiangge Nunnery

the Old Town, a few blocks from the Huangpu River. It is a working church, with Mass in Chinese said daily.
✚ K9 ✉ 185 Dongjiadu Lu 🚇 Nanpu Bridge 💷 Free

FUYOU MARKET

One of Shanghai's most well-known antiques markets, this place is at its busiest early on Sundays, but there's a permanent collection of stalls here that are open daily. Prices can be quite high, so haggling is a must.
✚ H7 ✉ 459 Fangbang Zhonglu 🕐 Daily 9–5 🍴 Restaurants 🚇 Yuyuan Garden 🚌 11, 14, 26, 66, 306 ♿ None 💷 Free

WEN MIAO

www.confuciantemple.com
Typical of Confucius temples with its main hall, the Dacheng Hall, dedicated to the sage, the few worshipers points to the decline of Confucianism, relative to Buddhism or Christianity; although the influence of Confucius in China is still immense. A used-book market is held on Sunday mornings.
✚ H8 ✉ 215 Wenmiao Lu 🕐 Daily 8.30–4.30 🚇 Laoximen 🚌 11, 14, 26 ♿ None 💷 Inexpensive

XIAOTAOYUAN MOSQUE

www.chinaislam.net.cn
Worth a visit to appreciate the multi-religious character of Shanghai, this small mosque was built in 1917.
✚ H8 ✉ 52 Xiaotaoyuan Lu 🕐 Daily, any time until 8.30pm 🚇 Laoximen

YUYUAN BAZAAR

www.yuyuantm.com.cn
Despite appearances—ceremonial gateways, rosewood lanterns, pagodas with sloping eaves—the Yuyuan Bazaar was built in the 1990s. This is one of the best places to shop for souvenirs, though not for genuine antiques. (Haggling is expected, but you may get a better price in the smaller shops on Fangbang Zhonglu.) Street artists entertain the crowds on summer weekends. Rows of stalls sell traditional snacks.
✚ J7 ✉ Streets around Yuyuan 🕐 Daily 7–6 🚇 Yuyuan Garden 🚌 26 ♿ None

Chopsticks at the Yuyuan Bazaar

The entrance to Yuyuan Bazaar

Old Town

Many old buildings remain in the Nanshi district, Shanghai's formerly walled Old Town, and you will see some of them on this walk.

DISTANCE: 1.5 miles (2.4km) **ALLOW:** 1 hour (not including stops)

START

DONGMEN LU
🚩 K8 🚌 55, 65

END

FUYOU MARKET
🚩 H7 🚇 Yuyuan Garden

❶ Start at Dongmen Lu, the site of the old east gate to the Chinese town, close to the Huangpu River. Walk westward and pass Waixiangua Jie (Salty Melon Street), with its local street market.

❼ Return to Jiujiaochang Lu, walk south to Fangbang Zhonglu and then turn right to browse through the shops of Old Street (▷ 78) and take a peek at the Fuyou Market (▷ 76), busiest on Sundays.

❷ Continue to Zhonghua Lu and cross the street to enter Fangbang Zhonglu.

❻ Turn left here and left again into Jiujiaochang Lu. A street on the right (Chenxiangge Lu) takes you to a small neighborhood temple, the Chenxiangge Nunnery (▷ 75).

❸ Continue past a variety of shops until an old Chinese arch appears to the right. This is the entrance to the Temple of the City God (▷ 75).

❺ Bear right around the lake and then turn left to wander among the narrow streets before bearing right to leave this area and emerge into Fuyou Lu.

❹ Go through the arch and make your way among the shops and restaurants until you come to the lake and the Huxinting Tea House (▷ 70–71), near the entrance to the Yuyuan (Yu Garden; ▷ 74).

OLD TOWN/NANSHI WALK

Shopping

DONGTAI LU ANTIQUES MARKET

With its stalls overflowing with fascinating Cultural Revolution knickknacks and any number of reproduction antiques, you won't necessarily find anything of great worth here (although you could be lucky), but rummaging through the stalls is endlessly absorbing. It's also a great place to pick up last-minute gifts and souvenirs, but remember this is a tourist market, so haggling is imperative.

➕ G7　✉ Dongtai Lu
🕓 Daily 9–5　🚇 Laoximen
🚌 13, 42, 63

FUMIN SMALL COMMODITIES MARKET

Located just outside the Yu Garden, this building houses a range of small shops that sell a wide variety of Chinese products.

➕ J7　✉ 223–225 Fuyou Lu　🕓 Daily 9–6　🚇 Yuyuan Garden　🚌 26

HUABAO BUILDING ANTIQUES MARKET

Housed in the basement of a building close to the Yu Garden, this is one of the city's best sources of quality antiques and knickknacks, so leave plenty of time to explore this little treasure trove.

➕ J7　✉ 265 Fangbang Zhonglu　🕓 Daily 9–5.30　🚇 Yuyuan Garden　🚌 42, 64

SHANGHAI OLD STREET

Not nearly as old as its name implies, having been redeveloped as recently as 1999, the eastern segment of Fangbang Zhonglu at least creates a fairly convincing illusion of being old, thanks to its small shops selling antiques, crafts, bric-a-brac and tea.

➕ J7　✉ Fangbang Zhonglu　🚇 Yuyuan Garden　🚌 26

SHILIUPU FABRIC MARKET

The former Dongjiadu market has moved

BUYING ANTIQUES

It is illegal to export anything older than 150 years. A red seal on an antique will tell you that it is genuine and exportable. There are so many shops and market stands selling antiques that the seal of approval may be absent, and if it is, there's no sure-fire method of knowing what you are buying other than to really inspect the object in question. Some imitations are of a very high standard but are often marked on the bottom as being authentic reproductions. This is information the salesperson is unlikely to volunteer, but if you like the item it will still be cheaper than the real thing!

---

around since closing several years ago and recently came to these indoor premises in the Old Town. There's a large selection of raw textiles to choose from (wool, silk, linen, cotton and others), sold from scores of stalls. You can also have clothes made to measure here, although you may have to hunt around to find someone who speaks English.

➕ J8　✉ 168 Dongmen Lu　🕓 Daily 9– 6.30　🚇 Yuyuan Garden

SILK WORLD

This emporium on the edge of the Yuyuan Bazaar sells all manner of silk products, from shirts and jackets to quilts and embroidered pyjamas.

➕ J7　✉ 125 Jiujiaochang Lu　☎ 2302 9374　🕓 Daily 9–5.50　🚇 Yuyuan Garden　🚌 26

SOUTH BUND FABRIC MARKET

A wonderful labyrinth of stalls laden with every type of material from wool, cotton and linen to silk and cashmere, this famous market is the place to go if you are after an inexpensive suit or dress. Tailors are on hand to measure you there and then while seamstresses will run up the garment in 24 hours if you need it that quickly.

➕ J9　✉ 399 Lujiabang Lu　☎ 6377 2236　🕓 Daily 9–6　🚇 Nanpu Bridge

Restaurants

PRICES

Prices are approximate, based on a 3-course meal for one person.

$$$	more than 250RMB
$$	100–250RMB
$	under 100RMB

HUXINTING TEA HOUSE ($)

www.yuyuantm.com.cn
There's nowhere in Shanghai quite like this venerable teahouse (▷ 70) for experiencing a taste of Old China, even if popularity has brought in the crowds.
🚹 J7 ✉ 257 Yuyuan Lu ☎ 6373 6950 🕐 Mon–Fri 8.30am–9.30pm, Sat–Sun 8am–10pm 🚇 Yuyuan Garden 🚌 14, 26

LAO FANDIAN (SHANGHAI OLD RESTAURANT; $$–$$$)

www.yuyuantm.com.cn
Something of an institution, this modernized version of an old restaurant (the name means "old restaurant") serves Shanghai dishes (including noodles, and seafood according to the season) and is conveniently situated in the Old Town.
🚹 J7 ✉ 242 Fuyou Lu ☎ 6311 1777 🕐 Daily lunch, dinner 🚇 Yuyuan Garden 🚌 26

LU BO LANG ($$)

International movers and shakers, celebrities and ordinary folk alike pile into this signature Old Town traditional eatery on the edge of the Yuyuan lake. Celebrity status has made the Shanghainese food a little touristy and the bills higher, but the experience is worthwhile.
🚹 J7 ✉ 115 Yuyuan Lu ☎ 6328 0602 🕐 Daily 7.30am–8.15pm 🚇 Yuyuan Garden 🚌 26

NAN XIANG ($–$$)

The best place in the city to try xiaolongbao (Shanghai-style steam dumplings). These are stuffed with various fillings: vegetables, crab, pork. All three floors here are usually busy, so be ready to wait for a table.
🚹 J7 ✉ 85 Yuyuan Lu ☎ 6355 4206 🕐 Daily lunch, dinner 🚇 Yuyuan Garden 🚌 26

LOCAL SNACKS

One of the specialties of the region is Ningbo or "pigeon egg" dumplings, little balls of sticky rice enclosing a delicious sweet osmanthus paste. Another snack is zhong zhi, sticky rice with meat wrapped in a lotus leaf. To find these and other delicious snacks, stop in the Old Town—both in the area of the Huxinting Tea House (🚹 J7 🚌 26) and on the streets around it, where there are many small restaurants and stalls.

OLD SHANGHAI TEA HOUSE ($)

Escape the busyness of the Yuyuan Bazaar to this small island of peace and sanity. The teahouse is awash with 1920s memorabilia, with everything from cookie tins to old telephones. The staff wear Mandarin gowns or silk qipaos and serve the teas on lacquered trays. Snacks of sour plums, muskmelon seeds and quail eggs come with the tea.
🚹 J7 ✉ 385 Fangbang Zhonglu ☎ 5382 1202 🕐 Daily 9–9 🚌 42, 66, 969

SHANGHAI CHIC ($$)

Authentic Shanghai cuisine in a stylish restaurant a short walk from Fuyou Market and Yuyuan Bazaar. The food is very good, with the pork ribs one of the star items, but service can be patchy.
🚹 H8 ✉ 5th floor, 489 Henan Nanlu ☎ 6335 7778 🕐 Daily 11–2.30, 5–9.30 🚇 Yuyuan Garden 🚌 26

SONGYUELOU ($)

Dating back to 1910, this is one of Shanghai's best-known vegetarian restaurants, cooking up a range of mock-meat dishes (the traditional way vegetarian food is prepared here). Dishes are inexpensive, and tasty.
🚹 J7 ✉ 99 Jiujiaochang Lu ☎ 6355 3630 🕐 Daily 11am–7.30pm 🚇 Yuyuan Garden 🚌 26

A rambling district north of Suzhou Creek, Hongkou incorporates the International Concession. It later became a haunt of liberal and revolutionary writers, artists and intellectuals.

Duolun Lu Cultural Street

● *Shikumen* houses
● Shops selling antiques, art and period bric-a-brac
● Bustling modern Chinese character and colonial-period mansions
● Atmospheric cafés

● The proximity of Duolun Lu and Lu Xun Park to each other and their complementary character should add up to a decent day out in old Hongkou.

This restored pedestrian street of *shikumen* houses and pebble-dash villas was once the haunt of China's radical writers. Now it is lined with art galleries, curio shops, teahouses and terrace cafés.

Shopping Take Metro line 3 to Dongbaoxing Road, turn right out of the station, then left onto Sichuan Beilu, and a five-minute walk brings you to Duolun Lu, where many of the shops specialize in collectibles. You can find antiques and knickknacks at No. 181 and collectible stones at No.189. Have a coffee among movie memorabilia at the Old Film Café (No. 123) or check out clocks at the Shanghai Nanjing Bells Collection Museum (No. 193) and chopsticks dating back to the Ming Dynasty at the Shanghai Chopsticks Museum (No.191).

From left to right: Great Virtue Church; a statue of Charlie Chaplin at the Old Film Café; people strolling along Duolun Lu Cultural Street

Culture You can photograph the old brick doorways, the clock tower and the former Great Virtue Church (No. 59), with its intriguing mixture of Chinese and Western styles. The church now houses small craft shops, or you can check out the exhibitions in the Shanghai Duolun Museum of Modern Art.

Literary connections Bronze statues dotted along the street commemorate the coterie of radical liberal and Communist writers who met here in the 1930s, and who, between them, created a new Chinese literature, far removed in spirit from the fossilized tropes of the past. The most famous of them, Lu Xun, had a profound influence on Chinese literature and is still revered today. You can find out more about him by visiting the museum in Lu Xun Park (▷ 86).

THE BASICS

➕ K2
✉ South of Lu Xun Park and south of Tian'ai Lu, branching west off Sichuan Beilu
🚇 Dongbaoxing Road
🚌 4, 9, 18, 21
🍴 Cafés and teahouses

Shanghai Duolun Museum of Modern Art
www.duolunart.com
✉ 27 Duolun Lu
☎ 6587 6902
🕐 Tue–Sun 10–6
💰 Inexpensive

Lu Xun Park

The boating lake (left); locals playing Chinese chess (right)

THE BASICS

🔆 K–L1

✉ 146 Jiangwan Lu

🕐 Daily 6am–6pm

🍴 Snacks sold at stands in the park

🚇 Hongkou Stadium

🚌 18, 21

♿ None

🎟 Free

HIGHLIGHTS

● Lu Xun's mausoleum and Memorial Hall
● Boating lake

TIP

● Hongkou Stadium adjoins Lu Xun Park on the west side, making it possible to combine a soccer match with a visit to the park.

If you want a window on Shanghai life away from the city center, then try to get to Lu Xun Park, where local people come to find refuge and meet friends away from their crowded housing conditions.

Hongkou Hongkou is the area north of Suzhou Creek (the Wusong River), a large part of which was the former American Concession before it merged with the British Concession in 1863. The accepted date of its foundation is 1848, when a church mission was established here. After the Americans, Hongkou became home to many Japanese, earning the soubriquet of Little Tokyo. Here also was the Mixed Court (administered by a Chinese magistrate and a foreign assessor), the Russian post office and various risqué cabarets.

Lu Xun Lu Xun Park, originally laid out in 1905, has a large lake with rowing boats for hire in the summer. Shrubs and flowers attract butterflies, while the open-air setting draws amateur painters and opera singers. Every autumn there are chrysanthemum shows. Above all, the park is known for its associations with the eminent writer Lu Xun, who lived in Hongkou from 1927 until his death in 1936, and is best known for *The True Story of Ah Q*, which lampoons the Chinese character. His house, at 9 Dalu Xinchun, Sanyin Lu, on a street just outside the park, is open to the public and illustrates what housing was like in the Japanese part of Shanghai. In the park there is a museum dedicated to his life, as well as his mausoleum and his likeness cast in bronze.

Shopping

DIAO YI DIAO SWAP SHOP

An Aladdin's cave of objets d'art, curios, porcelain, and assorted antiques which, despite the shop's name, you can also haggle over.

➕ J1 ✉ 145 Tongming Lu ☎ 2174 7665 🕐 Daily 12–8 🚇 Hongkou Stadium 🚌 132, 139

GUO CHUN XIANG CURIOSITY SHOP

Some of the objects on sale in this cluttered little shop are antiques, but "collector's items" might be a better way to describe the curios, minor pieces, pop-culture items, Mao badges, toys and Chinese bric-a-brac from as recently as the 1960s.

➕ K2 ✉ 179–181 Duolun Lu ☎ 5696 3948 🚇 Dongbaoxing Road 🚌 17, 18, 19, 21, 70

HONGKOU PLAZA

www.capitamallsasia.com
Opened at the beginning of 2012, this eight-story shopping, dining, entertainment, and lifestyle complex is located right by the Hongkou Football Stadium; it offers shoppers unrivaled transport links. Anchored by Carrefour, it features a mix of international and Chinese brand stores, while dining options range from snacks to high-end cuisine.

➕ K1 ✉ 388 Xijiang Wanlu ☎ 2601 9088 🕐 Daily 10–10 🚇 Hongkou Stadium 🚌 132, 139

QIPU MARKET

Huge clothing market with piles of items at knock-down prices; get your elbows out and haggle hard.

➕ J4 ✉ Qipu Lu 🕐 Daily 9–5 🚇 Baoshan Road

Restaurants

AFANTI RESTAURANT ($)

There are several excellent Uiguir/Muslim restaurants in town and this is one of the best. Don't be put off by the unimpressive interior. The food—largely grilled lamb—hits the spot. When you have had enough Shanghai food, this is a great place for naan bread, kebabs (yangrouchuan) and cuisine from northwest China's Central Asian-Silk Road frontier-land.

➕ Off map ✉ Tianshan Hotel, 775 Quyang Lu ☎ 6555 9604 🕐 Daily 9am–10pm 🚇 Chifeng Road

HONG GUAN ($$)

This is the place to dine if you are looking for well-cooked Cantonese cuisine and expertly prepared dim sum, as they are both on offer at this restaurant, which is conveniently close to Hongkou Stadium and Lu Xun Park.

➕ K1 ✉ 444 Dongjiangwan Lu ☎ 5696 6338 🕐 Daily 10.30–2.30, 4.30–9.30 🚇 Hongkou Stadium 🚌 18, 70, 502

KEN'S KITCHEN ($–$$)

International fare is served up in this unassuming restaurant, in a lovely colonial-era villa at the southern end of Hongkou. Signature dishes include baked sea bass and chicken with curry fruit sauce.

➕ J4 ✉ 15 Kunshan Huayuan Lu ☎ 6306 9238 🕐 Daily 10am–10pm 🚇 North Sichuan Road 🚌 6, 13, 14, 52

Pudong is a city of 1.5 million people, typified by its skyscrapers, nocturnal neon lights and huge avenues. It sprang up from farmland in less than 20 years, becoming an icon of 21st-century China.

Hua

H u a

Binjiang

BUND SIGHTSEEING TUNNEL

Shanghai Natural Wild Insect Kingdom

Fenghe Lu

Shanghai International Convention Centre

Oriental Pearl Tower

YAN'AN DONGLU TUNNEL

Lujiazui Xilu

Lujiazui

Super Brand Mall

Riverside Park

PUDONG

Fucheng

Shangri La Hotel

Huanlu

Lujiazui

LAN NI DU

RENMIN LU TUNNEL

H u a n g p u

Huangpu

⑤
⑥
⑦
⑧
⑨

Ⓙ
Ⓚ

Oriental Pearl Tower

HIGHLIGHTS

● Spectacular views across the city
● A glimpse into the future of Shanghai

TIP

● There are several other places in Pudong where you can get similar views, including the world's second highest observation deck in the Shanghai World Financial Center (▷ 94) or the 88th-floor observation deck of the Jinmao Tower (▷ 94).

The Oriental Pearl Tower rises as a 1990s monument to China's gravity-defying ambitions, and it offers fantastic views across Shanghai. It is emblematic of Lujiazui—the new-fangled forest of high-rises visible across the Huangpu River from the Bund.

Sky-high Towering above the western end of Pudong is now the fastest-growing urban area in the world—the Oriental Pearl Tower is the third-tallest tower in Asia and the fifth-loftiest in the world (the world's second-tallest building, rather than tower, is the nearby Shanghai Tower, ▷ 94). Devoid of any natural grace and typical of the brash early 1990s that sent its concrete form skyward, the tower has nonetheless come to symbolize Shanghai.

Clockwise from left: The Pudong skyline and the Oriental Pearl Tower; Illuminated stairs of the Oriental Pearl Tower; there are superb vistas from both viewing platforms

Visiting the tower The vista over Shanghai and beyond from the viewing area halfway up is excellent. Beyond the views, the highlight of the tower is buried away in the basement: the Shanghai History Museum. Take a voyage through the pages of Shanghai's history, with particular emphasis on Shanghai's rise as a city under foreign control. Various ticket options are available, such as the Shanghai History Museum alone; the museum plus the middle sphere or all spheres; or the museum plus dinner.

The river A short walk away, the Riverside Promenade is an attractive counterpoint to the tower, with views alongside the Huangpu River across to the historic buildings of the Bund (▷ 58–59). Boat tours are available from the nearby dock situated to the north of the tower.

THE BASICS

www.orientalpearltower.com
➕ K6
✉ 1 Shiji Dadao
☎ 5879 1888
🕐 Daily 8am–9.30pm
🚇 Lujiazui
🚌 Bund Sightseeing Tunnel
🚢 Ferry from opposite Yan'an Donglu
♿ Moderate
💰 Moderate
Shanghai History Museum
☎ 5879 8888
💰 Moderate

Pudong Skyscrapers TOP 25

Inside the Jin Mao Tower (left); Jin Mao Tower, the world's 16th-tallest building (right)

THE BASICS

Jin Mao Tower
www.jinmao88.com
⊞ L7
✉ 88 Shiji Dadao (Century Avenue)
☎ 5047 6688
🍴 Restaurants and cafés
🚇 Lujiazui
🎫 Free

Shanghai World Financial Center
http://swfc-shanghai.com
⊞ L7
✉ 100 Shiji Dadao (Century Avenue)
🍴 Restaurants and cafés
🚇 Lujiazui
🎫 Free (charge for observation deck)

HIGHLIGHTS

● Views from the Jinmao Tower's 88th-floor observation deck
● Views from the observation decks of the Shanghai World Financial Center
● Grand Hyatt Hotel's restaurants

TIP

● Have a drink in the top-floor bar, Cloud 9, in the Grand Hyatt Hotel (▷ 112) in the Jin Mao Tower; it is one of the world's highest..

Pudong's financial district is Asia's fastest growing. Of the more than 6,000 skyscrapers in Shanghai, many of them crowd here. The effect is both dwarfing and dazzling, and there are ample opportunities to climb into the clouds for some excellent views.

Jin Mao Tower A Chinese pagoda inspired the design of this soaring edifice, completed in 1999 and now the 16th tallest in the world, at 1,380ft (420m). On clear days the 88th-floor observation deck gives spectacular views of Shanghai. You can send a postcard direct from the Post Office. After dark, enjoy views of the city's lights and the gourmet restaurants of the Grand Hyatt Hotel (▷ 112), occupying floors 53 through 87.

Shanghai World Financial Center Shaped like a bottle opener, this 1,614ft-high (492m) tower is the seventh-tallest building in the world. Completed in 2008, it is home to one of the world's highest hotels, the Park Hyatt Shanghai. There are three observation decks in the SWFC, on the 94th, 97th, and 100th floors (the latter is the second-highest observation deck in the world).

Shanghai Tower Topped out in early 2014 and expected to open in 2015, Shanghai's newest skyscraper is now the second-tallest building in the world, and China's tallest, at 2,073ft (632m). The tower twists 120 degrees from base to tip and its 121 occupied floors will include shops, offices, entertainment, a luxury hotel, cultural venues, and an observation deck.

More to See

CENTURY PARK

www.centurypark.com.cn

Here you'll find a lake (where you can rent boats), gardens, pavilions and children's play areas. And a river, the Zhangjiabang, runs through it.

🚹 Off map, east of M8 ✉ Huamu Lu and Jinxiu Lu ☎ 3876 0588 🕐 Daily 7–6 (until 5 mid-Nov to mid-Mar) 🚇 Century Park ♿ Good 💷 Inexpensive

LUJIAZUI GREEN

This large, tree-fringed garden with a lake at its heart is popular with the workers of Pudong's many offices.

🚹 L6 ✉ Lujiazui Lu 🕐 24 hours 🚇 Lujiazui ♿ Good 💷 Free

SHANGHAI ANIMATION & COMICS MUSEUM

In Pudong's Zhangjiang Hi-Tech Park, this museum comprises three floors telling the story of animation as well as interactive activities.

🚹 Off map, east of M8 ✉ 69 Zhangjiang Lu ☎ 5895 7998 🕐 Tue–Sun 10–5 🚇 Jinke Road, then taxi 🚌 609, 961, 977 ♿ Few 💷 Moderate

SHANGHAI OCEAN WORLD AQUARIUM

www.sh-aquarium.com

There are over 450 species here. It's the sharks, penguins and spider crabs that draw the crowds, but this is a rare chance to see endangered Chinese species. You can walk through the longest glass tunnel in the world (509ft/155m).

🚹 L6 ✉ 1388 Lujiazui Huanlu ☎ 5877 9988 🕐 Daily 9–6 (until 9 Jul and Aug); animal feeding times 9.45–11.10, 2.15–3.40 🚇 Lujiazui ♿ Few 💷 Expensive

SHANGHAI SCIENCE AND TECHNOLOGY MUSEUM

www.sstm.org.cn

This state-of-the-art museum, the largest of its kind in Asia, opened to popular acclaim in 2001. The scope of the exhibition extends from biodiversity and space exploration to design innovation and digital technology.

🚹 Off map at M8 ✉ 2000 Shiji Dadao (Century Avenue) ☎ 6862 2000 🕐 Tue–Sun 9–5.15 🚇 Shanghai Science and Technology Museum ♿ Few 💷 Expensive

The beautiful flower beds at Century Park

Shopping

CHIA TAI DEPARTMENT STORE

This branch of the Thai department store chain, on four floors of the Super Brand Mall, had a shaky start as shoppers were slow to take to Pudong. That has changed now that the store stocks a broader range of goods and the parent mall has reached a wider audience.

➕ K6 ✉ 168 Lujiazui Lu ☎ 6887 7888 🕐 Daily 10–10 🚇 Lujiazui

WAL-MART SUPERCENTER

www.wal-martchina.com
This branch of the US chain store, one of ten in Shanghai, is at the south end of Pudong's main development zone, near the Nanpu Bridge approach road.

➕ Off map at L9 ✉ 252–262 Linyi Beilu ☎ 5094 5881 🕐 Daily 9am–10pm 🚇 Tangqiao

YATAI SHENGHUI SHOPPING CENTRE

This mall below the Metro station at the Shanghai Science and Technology Museum (▷ 95) sells a range of modestly priced goods, from clothing to jewelry. It was known as the place to buy imitation branded goods, but authorities have cracked down on that.

➕ Off map at M9 ✉ 2002 Shiji Dadao (Century Avenue) ☎ 6854 2269 🕐 Daily 10–7 🚇 Science and Technology Museum

> ### SLOW START
>
> Pudong has been slow to take off as a shopping district. This is because shoppers have been slow to change their habits. Now, as more people settle in Pudong, and as the effects of the generally high level of disposable income of people living and working in Pudong have kicked in, the picture is changing. Retailers, large and small, cheap and expensive, are moving in.

Restaurants

> ### PRICES
>
> Prices are approximate, based on a 3-course meal for one person.
> $$$ more than 250RMB
> $$ 100–250RMB
> $ under 100RMB

DANIELI'S ($$–$$$)

www.starwoodhotels.com
Ultra-urbane Italian cuisine is served in a restaurant with dark, cherrywood decor near the top of the St. Regis Hotel (▷ 112). Look for innovative dishes made with yummy homemade pastas, truffles, porcini mushrooms and more. You can also enjoy the fine views.

➕ Off map at M9 ✉ St. Regis Hotel, 889 Dongfang Lu ☎ 5050 4567 🕐 Daily lunch, dinner 🚇 Century Avenue

JADE ON 36 ($$$)

www.shangri-la.com
This exceptional restaurant, on the 36th floor of the Shangri-La hotel's stunning Tower Two, is a gem of intercontinental, multicultural fusion in a setting of modernist Chinese themes.

➕ K6 ✉ Pudong Shangri-La Hotel, 33 Fucheng Lu ☎ 6882 8888 🕐 Daily 6pm–10.30pm 🚇 Lujiazui

LA VERBENA ($–$$)

www.laverbena.com.cn
Glass-sided Spanish restaurant serving up Catalan tapas right on the banks of the Huangpu River with an outside terrace offering superb views across to the Bund.

➕ K6 ✉ 2967 Lujiazui Xilu ☎ 5836 7977 🕐 Daily 11.30am–2am 🚇 Lujiazui

Other attractions lie a little bit farther from the heart of the city, but are still easy to reach and provide another dimension to a trip to Shanghai. With most sights busy on weekends, weekday trips are advised for eluding the crowds.

Expo Site

HIGHLIGHTS

● Art collections
● Stunning architecture
● Shanghai Biennale art show

TIP

● Take a ferry to visit the Expo Site, so that you can enjoy views of Shanghai's burgeoning skyline along the way.

The 1,300-acre site for China's first world's fair, Expo 2010—attended by a record-breaking 73 million people over six months—is now a cultural hub, with exhibition buildings reborn as arts and performance venues, and more.

Cultural epicenter Echoing the Expo 2010 theme, "Better City, Better Life," the sprawling site is fast becoming Shanghai's cultural epicenter. Among iconic pavilions transformed into cultural havens, the former Expo Cultural Center where the opening ceremony was staged is now the Mercedes-Benz Arena, with an 18,000-seat auditorium hosting concerts by Chinese and international stars. Eight former Expo buildings have become Chocolate Happy Land, a wacky theme park based around chocolate. There is also a riverside park.

Clockwise from top left: The one-kilometer-long Expo Axis; inside the business center in the Expo site; the main entrance of the site provides a huge commerce area

China Art Museum The bright red, striking building that was formerly the Expo's China Pavilion is the new home for part of the collection from the now-closed Shanghai Art Museum in People's Square and is also known as the China Art Palace. Its five floors have permanent displays of 20th-century Chinese paintings, augmented by temporary exhibitions covering art, photography, stone carvings, historic art treasures and other themes.

Power Station of Art Taking its cue from London's Tate Modern, this former power station across the Huangpu River from the main Expo site now pays homage to post-1980s art from China and around the world in its lofty interior, having been the Pavilion of the Future for the 2010 fair. Every two years it stages Shanghai Biennal contemporary art exhibition previously held at the Shanghai Art Museum.

THE BASICS

The 2010 Expo Site covers both sides of the Huangpu River, mostly in Pudong but also in Puxi.

China Art Museum
www.sh-artmuseum.org.cn
➕ Off map
✉ 205 Shangnan Lu
☎ 2025 2018
🕐 Tue–Sun 9–5 last entry 4pm
🍴 Café inside, restaurants and cafés nearby
Ⓜ China Art Museum
🚌 955
♿ Good
✋ Free; inexpensive for special exhibitions

Power Station of Art
www.powerstationofart.com
➕ Off map (south of Nanshi)
✉ 200 Huayuangang Lu
☎ 3110 8550
🕐 Daily 11–7
🍴 Restaurants and café
Ⓜ South Xizang Road
🚌 65, 928
♿ Good
✋ Moderate for special exhibitions

Jade Buddha Temple

HIGHLIGHTS

● Active temple
● Beautiful jade carvings

TIPS

● The temple is home to a famous vegetarian restaurant where you can enjoy tasty Chinese Buddhist meat-free dishes. As is the Buddhist way, food is prepared to resemble the texture of meat.
● Photographing either of the jade Buddha statues in the temple is not permitted.

Shanghai's most famous temple stands among high-rise buildings in the north of the city. The highlight of a visit to this small Buddhist shrine is its Jade Buddha in the library and the surrounding atmosphere of veneration and devotion.

The temple The Jade Buddha Temple (Yufo Si) is one of Shanghai's few historic Buddhist temples. It was established in 1882 by a monk from the sacred Buddhist mountain of Putuoshan (the home of the Buddhist Goddess of Mercy), in Zhejiang province, to house the jade figures. Abandoned after the fall of the Qing dynasty in 1911 and then restored between 1918 and 1928, the temple has endured the vicissitudes of the 20th century but has been well preserved. It is certainly not one of China's largest, but is an impressive example of the

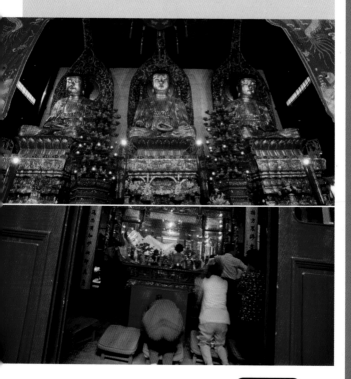

Clockwise from top left: Lighting candles from an open flame; a young woman raises a lighted candle; three Buddhas in the temple complex; worshipers at prayer in the temple; dragon detail on the facade; a huge incense burner in the courtyard

South Chinese style, especially the roof of the main hall, with its steeply raised eaves and decorative figurines. The temple is particularly worth visiting on the first and fifth days of each month, holy days that attract many worshipers.

The Jade Buddhas The temple consists of several halls, including the impressive Hall of Heavenly Kings and the ornate Great Treasure Hall, with its three golden Buddhas. The highlights, however, are the two jade statues brought from Burma by Abbott Wei Ken, each carved from a single piece of creamy white jade and separately housed. The first is a 3ft-long (1m) reclining Buddha. The more beautiful figure is in the library; almost 6.5ft (2m) high, it weighs around 2,200 lb (1,000kg), is encrusted with semi-precious stones and emits a divine aura.

THE BASICS

✚ D3
✉ 170 Anyuan Lu, Putuo
☎ 6266 3668
🕐 Daily 8–5
🍴 Excellent vegetarian restaurant
🚌 24, 105, 106, 112
♿ None
💲 Inexpensive
❓ Regular services

Shanghai Zoo

Residents at the zoo range from birds to the ever-popular pandas

THE BASICS

www.shanghaizoo.cn

🚇 Off map to west

✉ Hongqiao, Hongqiao Lu (near airport)

🕐 Mar–Oct 7.30–5; Nov–Feb 7.30–4.30

🍴 Restaurants

🚌 57, 91, 519, 709, 748, 806, 807, 809, 911, 925, 936, 941

♿ Few

💰 Moderate

HIGHLIGHTS

● Giant pandas
● Polar bears
● Green lawns
● Play areas for children

In addition to its collection of creatures, Shanghai Zoo is one of the city's most pleasant expanses of greenery and parkland, making it a perfect day out.

Green space This is one of the few parts of Shanghai where you can lie down on the grass in the sun with a soft drink. There's more of a sense of parkland here than at many other of Shanghai's more synthetic "parks." And like most zoos, this is a fun and educational place for children and there are play areas scattered around, as well as a children's zoo. Unfortunately, living quarters for the animals are not the best. The authorities are constantly making improvements, but overall the zoo can hardly rank with large city zoos in Europe or the US. However, the zoo does cooperate with international schemes to preserve rare and endangered species.

Panda stars Needless to say, the pandas—both giant and lesser pandas—are the stars of the show here, and their compound is the best laid-out of all, covering an area of some 1,435sq ft (1,200sq m). It has an indoor and an outdoor area, with a rockery, a pond and trees. But pandas are far from being the zoo's only species. There are some 620 in total, ranging from butterflies to Asian elephants, and coming from all continents. Among them are Brazilian wolves, African chimpanzees, penguins, peacocks, tigers, koala bears, a polar bear, golden-haired and squirrel monkeys, gorillas, South American buffalo and Père David's (Milu) deer.

Excursions

HANGZHOU

Within easy reach of Shanghai, Hangzhou is one of China's top tourist destinations and a historic former capital city. It is renowned for its magnificent West Lake.

Most of Hangzhou's sights cluster around the West Lake at the heart of town. Jump on a rental bicycle and circumnavigate the lake; starting at the Mausoleum of Yue Fei and cycling eastward, you'll pass Gushan Island, the Baochu Pagoda (overlooking West Lake from the hills to the north), then cycle south to the Leifeng Pagoda and the Jingci Temple and return via the Su Causeway through the lake itself. You can also take a boat trip to Xiaoying Island and the Mid-Lake Pavilion.

Off in the west is Hangzhou's most famous temple, the magnificent Lingyin Temple, one of Buddhist China's most important shrines. Hangzhou's museums are all free. Make sure you visit the China Silk Museum (in Yuhuangshan Lu) and the China Tea Museum (in Longjing Lu).

Hangzhou's prosperity came from the Grand Canal, which linked south and north China, but the city was also the capital of the Southern Song dynasty. Today it is a green and attractive city.

THE BASICS

Distance: 105 miles (170km)
✚ Off map to southwest
🍴 Many restaurants and cafés
🚆 Fast trains run to Hangzhou in around 80 minutes from Shanghai South Railway Station
♿ Few facilities
❓ Stay overnight to make the most of your visit. Hangzhou is well-supplied with hotels, from the luxurious Grand Hyatt Regency (28 Hubin Lu, tel 0571-8779 1234) to numerous youth hostels, including the decent Mingtown Youth Hostel (101-11 Nanshan Lu, tel 0571-8791 8948), where you can also rent bicycles

SHE SHAN

She Shan is a hill with an imposing redbrick Catholic church known as "Our Lady of China" at the summit. Mass continues to be celebrated here in Latin.

Its origins go back to the mid-19th century, when a wave of xenophobia led to the construction of a small chapel on the remote hillside. An acting bishop of Shanghai, later forced to take refuge here, vowed that in return for protection he would build a church (the current one dates from 1925). May is a time for pilgrimages, when streams of people climb the hill paths, which represent the Via Dolorosa (the route Jesus took to his crucifixion). Next to the church is an observatory.

THE BASICS

Distance: 19 miles (30km)
✚ Off map to southwest, 6 miles (10km) north of Songjiang town
🚆 Train from Guilin Road station (on Metro line 9) direct to She Shan station
Church
☎ 5765 1521
🕐 Daily 9–5
🍴 Restaurants and cafés nearby
🎟 Free

THE BASICS

Distance: 62 miles (100km)
🏳 Off map to west
🍴 Restaurants and cafés
🚆 Regular fast trains take less than 30 minutes to reach Suzhou from Shanghai Railway Station
♿ Few facilities
❓ Bicycles can be rented at the Mingtown Youth Hostel (28 Pingjiang Lu, tel 0512 6581 6869)

SUZHOU

Suzhou is one of China's most well-known canal towns and its gardens are famed across the land.

The Garden of the Master of the Nets (off Shiquan Jie, in the south of town) shows how a compact space can give the illusion of size; the Humble Administrator's Garden (178 Dongbei Jie, in the north of town) is a far larger garden.

Suzhou also has some fine temples and pagodas, including the West Garden Temple (Xiyuan Lu), the North Temple Pagoda (Renmin Lu), the Twin Pagodas, the Temple of Mystery (Guanqian Jie) and the Hanshan Temple. The Ruiguang Pagoda, near the Grand Canal in the south of Suzhou, rises up alongside Pan Gate (also called Panmen Gate), part of the original city wall.

Suzhou's museums are also excellent. Suzhou Museum (204 Dongbei Jie), designed by I.M. Pei, is visually stunning. Also worth visiting are the Suzhou Silk Museum (2001 Renmin Lu) and the Kunqu Opera Museum (14 Zhongzhangjia Xiang). If you want to spend the night, there are various options, from youth hostels to five-star hotels.

THE BASICS

Distance: 19 miles (30km)
🏳 Off map to southwest
🍴 Restaurants and cafés
🚌 Regular buses from Shanghai sightseeing bus center at Shanghai Stadium

ZHUJIAJIAO

Zhujiajiao is a small canal town with a wealth of historic features and archetypal images of traditional China.

Although the settlement is much older, it wasn't until the Ming dynasty that Zhujiajiao emerged as a prosperous and well-to-do canal town. Much of the Ming and Qing dynasty layout and architecture survives in the old town and a meander round its alleys turns up countless surprises. The standout sight is the long, hump-backed span of the Fangsheng Bridge, dating from the 16th century. The Yuanjin Buddhist Temple is also fascinating, and worth hunting down is the Catholic Church of Ascension, dating to the mid-19th century. You can also take boat tours along the canal.

Shanghai has a superb choice of places to stay, from glittering five-star towers to crisply efficient business hotels, fashionable boutique hideaways, low-cost chain hotels and a growing band of youth hostels for the more budget-conscious.

Where to Stay

Introduction

While Shanghai is top-heavy with high-end hotels on either side of the Huangpu River, the mid-range and budget brackets are also expanding. Booking ahead is always wise.

Variety of Accommodations

Hotels with historic character are plentiful but are often lacking in international experience. There is a glut of five-star hotels of international quality and a growing band of intimate, fashionable boutique hotels. The English-language skills of staff are generally satisfactory at five-star hotels, but can be lacking even in four-star establishments; staff attitudes can be another problem and the nuances of attentive international service can be curiously absent. There's a mushrooming band of well-located youth hostels, which tend to have young and fluent English-speaking staff and offer inexpensive but comfortable double rooms.

Location

The most fashionable areas are around the Bund, Nanjing Lu, People's Square and the French Concession. Pudong is awash with high-end hotels, but—apart from the excellent views from high-rise hotels—has little charm.

Room Prices

Prices are fast approaching European levels. Book online to secure a good deal. The official rate is hardly ever levied, except perhaps during the May 1 and October 1 holiday periods.

STARS IN THEIR COURSES

The hotel star-rating system employed in China can often be a reliable guide to what you can expect from a hotel, but not always, and may even be misleading in some cases. The nationally determined five-star category generally means what it says, though many hotels that are a decade or two old have never seen any modernization or upgrading, or even a lick of paint, since they were built. Four- and three-star hotels might have been "assisted" to their status by a "sympathetic" local official. Two- and one-star hotels can be surprisingly dowdy and may even have safety issues.

Budget Hotels

PRICES

Expect to pay under 700RMB for a double room per night for a budget hotel.

CAPTAIN HOSTEL

www.captainhostel.com.cn
A few steps from the Bund, the old-timer Captain is still going strong, with clean dorms and a fantastic roof-top bar offering staggering views as you enjoy a drink. Pass on the double rooms, but location-wise, this old sea dog is hard to beat.

➕ J6 ✉ 37 Fuzhou Lu
☎ 6325 5053 🚇 Nanjing Road (E)

EAST ASIA HOTEL

www.jinjianginns.com
In a historic building on Nanjing Donglu, the East Asia Hotel has long been a decent budget standby in the best part of the city. The area can be noisy—this is Nanjing Donglu after all—but you are right at the heart of the action. Check rooms first as they vary and some are noisier than others, depending on which direction they face.

➕ H5 ✉ 680 Nanjing Donglu ☎ 6322 3223
🚇 Nanjing Road (E)

ETOUR YOUTH HOSTEL

www.yhachina.com
The People's Square perch is fantastic and the main draw, but the architecture and courtyard feel of this place are big bonuses. Rooms are clean, but some are on the small side.

➕ G6 ✉ 55 Jiangyin Lu
☎ 6327 7766 🚇 People's Square

FISH INN

www.fishinn.com.cn
Boutique hotel with 30 rooms in a traditional shikumen area next to Suzhou Creek and just a few minutes' walk from Nanjing Lu's shops and the Bund. Don't expect too many niceties but the rooms are clean and each has a traditional theme.

➕ J5 ✉ 639 Henan Zhonglu
☎ 6324 2210 🚇 Nanjing Road (E)

MOTEL 168

www.motel168.com
If you're looking for a clean and modern hotel aimed at the lower end of the Chinese business market, chain hotel Motel 168 is excellent value.

➕ Off map ✉ 1119 West Yan'an Lu ☎ 5118 0999
🚇 Jiangsu Road

RESERVATIONS

If you are on a tight budget, it is best not to arrive in Shanghai without a hotel reservation. Budget accommodations are in fairly short supply, and wandering about this huge city with luggage could prove time consuming and expensive.

PARK HOTEL

www.internationalshotel.com
The Park Hotel is a classic prewar skyscraper, modernized a little garishly. It has an excellent location and facilities, which include a business area, shopping arcade, beauty salon and several restaurants.

➕ G5 ✉ 170 Nanjing Xilu
☎ 5180 1133 🚇 Renmin Park/People's Square
🚌 20, 37

SEVENTH HEAVEN

www.7hotel.cn
In a distinctive prewar building on Nanjing Lu, Seventh Heaven offers reasonable prices. Rooms are fairly well equipped and hotel facilities include a business center, post office and a number of restaurants, including Cantonese and Sichuan options.

➕ H5 ✉ 627 Nanjing Donglu ☎ 6322 0777
🚇 People's Square 🚌 37

LE TOUR TRAVELER'S REST YOUTH HOSTEL

www.letourshanghai.com
This spacious and well-run youth hostel is quietly buried away down a typical Shanghai alleyway in the Jing'an area. Rooms are pleasant, the staff are friendly, and there's table tennis, bike rental and a room for watching movies.

➕ C5 ✉ No. 36, Lane 319, Jiaozhou Lu ☎ 6267 1912
🚇 Changping Road

Mid-Range Hotels

PRICES

Expect to pay between 700 and 1,500RMB for a double room per night for a mid-range hotel.

ASTOR HOUSE HOTEL
www.astorhousehotel.com
Astor House offers a taste of concession-era Shanghai, with huge rooms and a sense of grandeur, all within walking distance of the Bund.
➕ K5 ✉ 15 Huangpu Lu ☎ 6324 6388 🚇 Tiantong Road 🚌 28

BROADWAY MANSIONS HOTEL
www.broadwaymansions.com
Renovated with a crisp new interior, this art deco hotel has a fantastic position, with views of the Huangpu River and Lujiazui, while overlooking Suzhou Creek and Waibaidu Bridge.
➕ K5 ✉ 20 Suzhou Beilu ☎ 6324 6260 🚇 Tiantong Road

CENTRAL HOTEL
www.centralhotelshanghai.com
This popular hotel, with WiFi, was renovated in 2011 and offers good value close to the Bund.
➕ H5 ✉ 555 Jiujiang Lu ☎ 5396 5000 🚇 Nanjing Road (E)

CYPRESS
www.jinjianghotels.com
About 1 mile (2km) from Hongqiao Airport and with a free shuttle bus to the city center, this modern hotel is set in gardens that give a sense of being in the country; you can even fish in a small lake. Rooms are functional but attractive.
➕ Off map ✉ 2419 Hongqiao Lu ☎ 6268 8868 🚌 91, 911, 925

HENGSHAN PICARDIE HOTEL
www.hengshanhotel.com
Restorations have brought a measure of class back to this art deco hotel—once the Picardie Apartments—on the French Concession edges. Excellent discounts are a further bonus.
➕ B8 ✉ 534 Hengshan Lu ☎ 6437 7050 🚇 Hengshan Road

HOTEL EQUATORIAL
www.equatorial.com
High-rise hotel, not far from the western part of Nanjing Lu, with a steak house, Italian, Cantonese and Japanese restaurants, and a 24-hour café. Also a gym, pool, sauna and tennis and squash courts.

BARGAINS

Hotels in Shanghai are expensive, but don't necessarily go by the official room rate, which hardly ever applies (except during busy holiday periods). Room rates are generally discounted by between 10 and 60 percent, so a hotel with luxury rates could turn out to be a far more affordable mid-range option.

➕ C6 ✉ 65 Yan'an Xilu ☎ 6248 1688 🚇 Jing'an Temple 🚌 57, 925

HOWARD JOHNSON HUAIHAI HOTEL SHANGHAI
http://huaihaishanghai.hojochina.com
A comfortable hotel in the heart of the French Concession with shops and restaurants a short stroll away– which makes up for the fact that the rooms are a bit tired and service is somewhat lacking.
➕ D7 ✉ 1 Fenyang Lu ☎ 5461 9898 🚇 Shanxi Road (S)

HYATT ON THE BUND
www.hyattonthebund.cn
It's not quite on the Bund, but the Hyatt's two towers have great views of the Bund and Pudong. The modern decor is stylish without going overboard, and rooms are spacious and cutting-edge.
➕ K5 ✉ 199 Huangpu Lu ☎ 6393 1234 🚇 Tiantong Road

JIN JIANG HOTEL
www.jinjianghotels.com
This art deco French Concession hotel is just off Huaihai Zhonglu, so sightseeing and shopping are a breeze. Rooms are in various buildings, with very different tariffs. There are excellent restaurants on-site and nearby.
➕ E7 ✉ 59 Maoming Nanlu ☎ 3218 9888 🚇 Shanxi Road (S)

MANSION HOTEL

www.mansionchinahotel.com
Former hangout of Green Gang boss Du Yuesheng, the Mansion Hotel conjures up the mood of 1930s Shanghai with its French Concession perch and period styling.
➕ D7 ✉ 82 Xinle Lu
☎ 5101 6060 🚇 Shanxi Road (S)

MARRIOTT HONGQIAO

www.marriott.com/shaqi
This family-friendly hotel offers excellent facilities at reasonable prices. Handy for Hongqiao Airport, it is also close to the Yan'an Expressway, with fast transit to the center. Rooms are spacious and tastefully furnished, and there's a gym and sauna.
➕ Off map ✉ 2270 Hongqiao Lu ☎ 6237 6000
🚌 911, 925, 936

NEW WORLD MAYFAIR HOTEL

www.newworldhotels.com
Efficient and neat, this business hotel offers views from its north side over Zhongshan Park. Although in the west of the city, it's next to Zhongshan Park Metro station for swift access to town on line 2.
➕ Off map ✉ 1555 Dingxi Lu ☎ 6240 8888
🚇 Zhongshan Park

NOVOTEL ATLANTIS

www.novotel.com
While it mimics the typical model of a large, business-oriented tower hotel, its ownership by a French chain affords the Atlantis some refreshing design and service touches. It's a bit isolated, but four restaurants, three bars, a pool and other amenities compensate.
➕ Off map ✉ 728 Pudong Dadao ☎ 5036 6666
🚇 Pudong Avenue

RADISSON HOTEL SHANGHAI NEW WORLD

www.radisson.com/shanghaicn_newworld
Rising over Renmin Park and People's Square, this modern tower—topped with a flying-saucer-style revolving restaurant—offers excellent value, first-rate views and a host of facilities, plus a high-altitude bar.
➕ G5 ✉ 88 Nanjing Xilu ☎ 6359 9999 🚇 People's Square

LODGING IN PUDONG

Pudong has a virtually complete absence of anything that remotely resembles traditional Chinese style. Twenty-first century Chinese style is something else. The fact that everything is shiny, international and new, and works, makes Pudong attractive in its own right. And it's easy enough to be whisked across the river by taxi, shuttle bus or limousine, or by Metro or ferry, to be back where the action is.

RUIJIN GUEST HOUSE

www.ruijinhotelsh.com
Guests stay in five redbrick villas—mostly dating from the 1920s—in the grounds of the former Morris Estate. The setting is simply stunning: Within a walled enclosure are a Japanese garden, a small lake and manicured lawns. The tasteful rooms are a good size; some have balconies overlooking the garden.
➕ E8 ✉ 118 Ruijin 2-Lu
☎ 5180 1144 🚇 Shanxi Road (S)

SHERATON SHANGHAI HONGQIAO HOTEL

www.starwoodhotels.com
This comfortable hotel is convenient for the airport. There are six restaurants, a health club and a business center.
➕ Off map ✉ 5 Zunyi Lu
☎ 6275 8888 🚌 57

TAIYUAN VILLA

www.ruijinhotelsh.com
This elegant and comfortable French-Renaissance-style mansion is set in a secluded garden, and formerly belonged to US general George Marshall. Most of the accommodations are in villas around the mansion. The hotel has few facilities, but there are plenty of bars and restaurants nearby.
➕ D8 ✉ 160 Taiyuan Lu
☎ 6471 6688 🚇 Hengshan Road

WHERE TO STAY MID-RANGE HOTELS

Luxury Hotels

PRICES

Expect to pay more than 1,500RMB per night for a double room.

GRAND HYATT

www.shanghai.grand.hyatt.com
Spectacular views are the preserve of the Hyatt, which takes the top 34 floors of the Jin Mao Tower (▷ 94). All rooms have floor-to-ceiling windows, but those facing the river are the most sought-after.
🔢 L7 ✉ 88 Shiji Dadao (Century Avenue) ☎ 5049 1234 🚇 Lujiazui

JIA

www.jiashanghai.com
The Hong Kong hotel name has come to Shanghai with this hip operation just off Nanjing Lu. In the lobby tongue-in-cheek design features create a stylish entrée to the uniquely cool rooms.
🔢 E5 ✉ 931 Nanjing Xilu ☎ 6217 9000 🚇 Nanjing Road (W)

OKURA GARDEN HOTEL SHANGHAI

www.gardenhotelshanghai.com
Close to Huaihai Zhonglu, this hotel sits behind the facade of the old French Club. It has five restaurants, including a Japanese one, a business area and health club.
🔢 E7 ✉ 58 Maoming Nanlu ☎ 6415 1111 🚇 Shanxi Road (S) 🚌 41

PARK HYATT

www.park.hyatt.com
Housed in the Shanghai World Financial Center (▷ 94), the Park Hyatt promises a luxurious and comfortable stay in Shanghai.
🔢 L7 ✉ 100 Shiji Dadao (Century Avenue) ☎ 6888 1234 🚇 Lujiazui

PEACE HOTEL

www.shanghaipeacehotel.com
This luxurious hotel is an Art Deco treasure, reinvented to cater for 21st-century visitors, with all the amenities and level of service you'd expect from one of Shanghai's premier hotels.
🔢 J5 ✉ 20 Nanjing Donglu ☎ 6321 6888 🚇 Nanjing Road (E) 🚌 27

THE PENINSULA SHANGHAI

www.shanghai.peninsula.com
Opened in 2009, this opulent hotel is the first new building on the Bund for seven decades and occupies a prime position, capitalized on with a rooftop terrace.
🔢 J5 ✉ 32 Zhongshan Dong 1-Lu ☎ 2327 2888 🚇 Nanjing Road (E) 🚌 65, 928

HOTEL SERVICE

Your hotel will offer one invaluable service apart from providing a room and shelter: Staff will write down your destination in Chinese for you to show to taxi drivers when you go out. Ask the doorman to make sure that the driver knows exactly where you want to go—and don't forget to take the hotel's own namecard with you for the return journey.

PORTMAN RITZ-CARLTON

www.ritzcarlton.com
This hotel—an intrinsic part of the Shanghai Centre—remains one of the most superior business hotels in Shanghai, in one of the best parts of town. Service, facilities and rooms are all top-notch and the overall presentation is simply excellent.
🔢 D5 ✉ 1376 Nanjing Xilu ☎ 6279 8888 🚇 Jing'an Temple 🚌 20, 37

PUDI BOUTIQUE HOTEL

www.boutiquehotel.cc
A delicious hotel—in the best part of the French Concession—offering seductive interior design and high levels of service.
🔢 F7 ✉ 99 Yandang Lu ☎ 5158 5888 🚇 Huangpi Road (S)

ST. REGIS

www.starwoodhotels.com
Regularly voted one of Asia's best hotels, the St. Regis is the ultimate in luxury with spacious rooms. Guests have access to their own butler 24 hours a day.
🔢 Off map at M9 ✉ 889 Dongfang Lu ☎ 5050 4567 🚇 Dongfang Lu

Use this section to help you plan your visit to Shanghai. We have suggested the best ways to get around the city and useful information for when you are there.

Need to Know

Planning Ahead

When to Go

The best time to visit Shanghai is either in late spring (April/May) or in early fall (late September to October), when days can be clear and warm and comfortable for exploring on foot. June and July are very hot and see occasional epic rainstorms; August is also very hot. Winter is miserable, damp and cold.

TIME

Shanghai is 13 hours ahead of New York and 8 hours ahead of the UK. Shanghai does not have daylight saving.

AVERAGE DAILY MAXIMUM TEMPERATURES

JAN	FEB	MAR	APR	MAY	JUN	JUL	AUG	SEP	OCT	NOV	DEC
45°F	46°F	50°F	64°F	73°F	79°F	88°F	86°F	77°F	72°F	61°F	50°F
7°C	8°C	10°C	18°C	23°C	26°C	31°C	30°C	25°C	22°C	16°C	10°C

Spring (March to May) is a pleasant time. The trees begin to blossom in April; May is usually comfortably warm but is often wet.

Summer (June to August) is extremely hot and humid, particularly July and August.

Autumn (September to October) is often pleasantly warm, although September is also one of the wetter months, and watch out for unexpectedly hot days.

Winter (November to February) is cold, clammy and overcast with occasional snow, but temperatures don't often fall below freezing. It can be an unpleasant time to be in Shanghai.

WHAT'S ON

The dates of traditional Chinese festivals vary from year to year according to the lunar calendar, which usually begins in February.

Winter/spring *Chinese New Year/Spring Festival*: The most important festival in the Chinese calendar usually falls in February. Red envelopes containing money are given to encourage prosperity. It's a festive time to be in the city, but getting tickets for journeys out of town can be tricky. *Lantern Festival* (15th day of the first lunar month): Locals eat *tangyuan* (sticky and

sweet dumplings), visit temples and may hang out paper lanterns.

Guanyin's Birthday (19th day of the second moon): Guanyin is the goddess of mercy, and on her birthday Buddhist temples are filled with worshipers.

Longhua Temple Fair (third lunar month): Celebrating the founding of Longhua Temple.

May *International Labor Day* (May 1): Three-day holiday. *Music Festival*: A festival of classical western and traditional music.

June *Children's Day* (Jun 1).

September *Mid-Autumn Festival* (15th day of the eighth moon): Recalls a 14th-century uprising against the Mongols and is now celebrated with Moon cakes, filled with lotus root, dates and sesame.

October *National Day* (Oct 1): Celebration of the founding of the People's Republic of China. Week-long holiday.

November *Shanghai Marathon*.

December *Christmas Day* (Dec 25): Increasingly a festive event in Shanghai.

Shanghai Online

www.shanghaidaily.com
The English online version of the *Shanghai Daily* presents a somewhat sober style and all the news the government thinks is fit to print. But it contains plenty of useful news, views and information about practical matters.

www.timeoutshanghai.com
Exhaustive details about forthcoming Shanghai events as well as listings for restaurants, bars, clubs, art galleries and attractions.

www.shanghai.gov.cn
The official website of the Shanghai Municipality has an extensive English section covering city news and services, travel, leisure and hotels.

www.shanghaihighlights.com
The Shanghai website of tour operator China Highlights. It features many guided-tour and excursion options in the city.

www.shanghaiist.com
One of the city's best general websites, aimed mainly at the young, footloose, fancy-free and ready-to-party.

www.smartshanghai.com
This hip site aims to get you to the coolest parties, raves, dance clubs and other venues where the action is hot and happening.

www.travelchinaguide.com
This comprehensive general China travel website covers cultural issues in Shanghai in reasonable depth, providing decent introductions to places of interest and practical matters. Note that some information is dated.

www.cityweekend.com.cn
Online companion to the twice-monthly magazine highlighting what's happening in Shanghai, with reader reviews and a classified section.

USEFUL TRAVEL SITE

www.fodors.com
A complete travel-planning site. You can research prices and weather; book air tickets, cars and rooms; pose questions to fellow travelers; and find links to other sites.

INTERNET CAFÉS

Amid official unease at the freedom Internet cafés give users to receive information and opinions (as well as concerns about young people becoming addicted to chatrooms and games), Internet cafés face strict controls and are often shut down. Increasing WiFi access in restaurants and hotels has also led to many closing. The Internet is subjected to censorship and controls in China, and you will need your passport in order to get online at Internet cafés.

Jinfeng Internet Bar
➕ Off map (Yangpu district)
✉ 1970 Pingliang Road
◎ 24 hours
🚇 Ningguo Road 🚌 28, 29

Shanghai Library
➕ C7–B7 ✉ 1555 Central Huaihai Zhonglu ☎ 6445 5555 ◎ Daily 8–8
🚇 Shanghai Library

Getting There

AIRPORT TAX

● 50RMB for domestic flights, 90RMB for international flights. These taxes are included in the price of air tickets.

ENTRY REQUIREMENTS

● Visitors must hold a valid passport with at least six months' validity.

● Visas for all foreign nationals must be obtained in advance from the nearest Chinese Consulate or Embassy. Tourist visas are generally valid for 30 days but can sometimes be extended in China. Allow up to five days for its issue. A passport photograph, completed application form and fee will be required. If in a group, you may be visiting on a group visa.

● In Shanghai, visa extensions are issued by the Public Security Bureau ⊠ 1500 Minsheng Lu, Pudong.

● No vaccinations are required unless you are coming from a yellow fever infected area. However, doctors may recommend certain precautionary measures.

NEED TO KNOW GETTING THERE

AIRPORTS

International flights arrive at Shanghai Pudong International Airport (PVG), 19 miles (30km) east of the city. Domestic flights use Pudong International Airport or Hongqiao International Airport, in the west of Shanghai.

40 miles (60km)

Hongqiao International **Pudong International**

ARRIVING BY AIR (INTERNATIONAL)

The website for Shanghai Pudong International Airport is www.shanghaiairport.com. At the airport, information counters are by the domestic and international security check areas and airside in the domestic departure area. There is a luggage storage facility in International Arrivals (☎ 96990 🕐 Daily 6am–midnight), as well as ATMs. The airport has a long-distance bus station for buses to Suzhou and Hangzhou. Transportation to Shanghai is by shuttle buses, taxi or Maglev, the world's first commercial Magnetic Levitation rail system. Shuttle buses leave every 10 to 30 minutes from Arrivals; the journey to central Shanghai takes from 40 minutes to an hour or more (seven routes). Buy tickets on board the bus. Taxi stands are to the right outside the Arrivals hall. Have your destination written in Chinese, and ensure the meter is switched on. Ignore the unofficial taxi touts in and just outside the Arrivals hall. A taxi trip will take 30–60 minutes, depending on traffic and your destination. Maglev trains traveling at up to 267mph (430kph) take less than 8 minutes to reach Longyang Road Metro station, on Metro Line 2. Maglev is accessed via level 2.

ARRIVING BY AIR (DOMESTIC)

For information about arriving at Pudong International Airport, ▷ opposite. Some domestic flights arrive at the older and far less efficient Hongqiao Airport, in the western suburbs. Both Arrivals halls at Hongqiao have hotel shuttle desks, and outside the halls are bus stops for buses to Shanghai Railway Station, Shanghai Stadium, People's Square, Pudong International Airport and other points. Taxis take 30–40 minutes to travel to the city center.

ARRIVING BY BOAT

Two companies operate services from Japan: The Shanghai Ferry Company, a weekly service from Osaka; and the Japan-China International Ferry Co., a weekly service from Kobe. Crossings take two days; ships dock at the International Passenger Terminal in Hongkou.

Most passengers arriving in Shanghai by boat do so on ferries from destinations on the East China Sea (Putuoshan) and the Yangtze River (Wuhan, Chongqing). These dock at the Wusong Passenger Terminal in the north of Shanghai or at Luchaogang in the south.

ARRIVING BY TRAIN

Most trains arrive at Shanghai Railway Station, in the north of town on Jiaotong Lu (some trains, for example from Hangzhou, arrive at Shanghai South Railway Station). Hold onto your ticket until you are out of the terminal. Taxis are readily available or you can hop onto Metro Line 1. If you don't have much luggage, the Metro is a better choice than taking a taxi, especially if you have a long journey. Resist the temptation to find a hotel in the area, as it has no charm. The station itself is large, complicated and swarming with people, so you won't want to hang around. It's easiest to try to book any outward train tickets through your hotel, for a small service charge, but remember to book days ahead. Getting hold of train tickets during the Chinese New Year, the May 1 and October 1 holiday periods can be very tricky.

CUSTOMS REGULATIONS

● You may import 400 cigarettes, 1.5 liters of alcohol, 0.5 liters of perfume.
● When departing, be careful that any antique you have purchased is permitted to leave the country. Antiques that are permitted for export must bear a red seal and any item not carrying the seal may be seized at customs.

VISITORS WITH DISABILITIES

China is not a country that has made many concessions to people with disabilities. However, very slowly, things are improving. As new hotels and museums are constructed, so access is being made easier for wheelchair users and wheelchairs are more readily available at airports. However, attitudes, in general, are not thoughtful or considerate—you should be prepared for difficulties and for the need to improvise.

INSURANCE

● Travel insurance covering medical expenses is essential.
● In the event of medical treatment, be sure to keep all receipts.

Getting Around

MAPS

Tourist maps of Shanghai are widely available from bookshops, hotels and tourist information centers.

WALKING BLUES

While getting around on foot is a great way to see the city, remember that distances are large and the streets are filled with pedestrians, traffic and noise. It can be exhausting, particularly in summer. It makes more sense to go by taxi or public transportation to the general area you want to explore and walk from there. Be cautious at all times when crossing roads, even at traffic lights. Shanghai's drivers show no mercy to mere pedestrians.

TAXI TRIALS

Many taxi drivers are from out of town and have only a superficial knowledge of Shanghai's roads. Take a look at the number of stars below the driver's photo on the dashboard; one is a beginner, five is an expert. Very few drivers speak English well, so have the address of your destination written down in Chinese. Avoid illegal taxis. Well-known taxi companies include Dazhong Taxi (☎ 96822) and Qiangsheng Taxi (☎ 6258 0000).

BICYCLES

● Bicycles (*zixing che*) are widely used and can be rented at little cost from some hotels or from specialist outlets. Bicycles are banned from some large roads in Shanghai, however.
● Check brakes and tires before setting out and observe how traffic functions in China—joining it unprepared can be an unnerving experience.

BUSES

● The comprehensive bus system is very inexpensive but buses can be crowded, especially during rush hour; buses are not foreigner-friendly, unless you can read Chinese.
● Buses run between 5am and 11pm.
● The best tourist bus routes are: the No. 11, which shuttles around the Old Town; the No. 930, which runs from the railway station past People's Square to Old Town and Dong Jia Du Lu; the No. 20, which travels from the Bund through People's Square to Jing'an Temple; and the No. 65, which runs between the Bund and close to the railway station.
● Make sure that you have small change—you pay your fare on board.
● Note that pushing your way on board is a feature of daily life. Pickpockets are not unknown.

FERRIES

● Ferries cross the Huangpu River between Pudong and the Bund from 7am to 10pm. Single fares are 2RMB.

METRO

● Shanghai's Metro network (www.shmetro. com) currently has 14 lines, and is the longest Metro system in China at more than 350 miles (563km). Still ambitiously expanding, the target is to expand the network to 373 miles (600km) in 2015 with more lines beyond that.
● The busiest station is People's Square, intersected by Lines 1, 2 and 8. Line 1 runs from Fujin Road in the north to Xinzhuang, via Shanghai Railway Station. Line 2 goes east from East Xujing Road to Pudong International

Airport, via the Maglev station at Longyang Road. Line 3 links North Jiangyang Road with Shanghai South Railway Station. Line 4 runs in a huge loop, linking Puxi and Pudong. Another useful line is Line 8, running from Yaohua Road in Pudong through People's Square to Shiguang Road.

● Trains run every few minutes from 5.30 or 6 in the morning until 10.30 or 11 in the evening, and platform screens show the next two trains due. Signs and announcements are in English and Chinese.

● Fares range from 3RMB to 9RMB. Travel in the central area on Lines 1 and 2 costs from 3RMB to 4RMB. Single tickets can be bought from station concourse vending machines or at ticket windows. For multiple journeys, buy a Shanghai Public Transportation Card, an electronic smart card swiped on automated ticket barriers. Refundable cards costing 20RMB are available from stations and convenience stores and can be topped up as desired. The cards can also be used for buses, taxis, ferries, the Metro and the Maglev airport shuttle bus.

● Overcrowding is a problem during rush hour. Glass safety screens with sliding doors have been installed on some platform edges.

● Metro lines are being renamed. Each line number will be prefixed by a letter identifying it as an elevated light railway (L), a central business district subway (M) or suburbs (R).

TAXIS

● Taxis are widely available, metered and easy to flag down.

● Travel by taxi is quite inexpensive and definitely the best way of getting around, occasional traffic jams notwithstanding.

● In general, Shanghai taxi drivers are very honest. However, if you are dissatisfied take note of the license number displayed inside.

● Never accept an offer of a ride from a driver of an illegal taxi. There are plenty of legal taxis in the city.

RETURN ADDRESS

Always carry with you a card or handwritten note in Chinese stating your hotel name and address, and perhaps even directions for how to get there if it is not likely to be well known or in an easily identifiable location. This will be particularly useful for taxi drivers—but might also come in handy should you be involved in an accident or lose your wallet or handbag. An extension of this precaution would be to carry information in Chinese about any chronic medical condition you have or medicines you need to take.

SIDE TRIPS

Shanghai is within striking distance of several of China's most interesting small—by Chinese standards—cities: Suzhou (▷ 106; the city of classic Chinese gardens); Hangzhou (▷ 105; described by Marco Polo as paradise on earth); Nanjing (a former capital on the Yangtze, with historical tombs and other sights on forested hills above the river); and Wuxi (the most convenient gateway to Lake Tai/Taihu). All of these can be reached by organized tour, or by train from Shanghai. Have someone at your hotel write down your destination in Chinese.

Essential Facts

left sidebar (rotated)NEED TO KNOW ESSENTIAL FACTS

EMERGENCY NUMBERS

● Ambulance ☎ 120
● Fire ☎ 119
● Police ☎ 110

MONEY

RMB (Renminbi) is the currency of China. The basic unit is the yuan (often called "kuai" in spoken Chinese), made up of 10 jiao (often called "mao" in spoken Chinese), each of which is divided into 10 fen (rarely used). There are notes for 1, 2, 5, 10, 20, 50 and 100 yuan, and the smaller 1, 2 and 5 jiao. There are also coins for 1 yuan; 1 and 5 jiao; and 5 fen.

ELECTRICITY

● The power supply is 220V, 50 cycles AC.
● Plug types vary, the most common is the two-flat-pin type. It is worth taking an adaptor.

ETIQUETTE

● Avoid displays of anger and aggression. If you have a complaint, gentle, persistent questioning is the best way of dealing with it.
● Remember that China is an authoritarian country where unorthodox opinions are discouraged.
● Table etiquette depends on where you eat. Good table manners are essential in smart restaurants, and especially at banquets, but at cheaper restaurants chicken bones are flung on the floor and a pall of cigarette smoke hangs over loud-talking diners.

MEDICAL TREATMENT

● Treatment is available in state hospitals and in private, joint-venture clinics.
● For minor ailments, the foreigner section of the state-run hospitals will normally be the cheapest option. However, try to ascertain the cost of treatment in advance.
● Your host organization (eg. CITS) or hotel will help to put you in contact with a hospital.
● Private clinics: Shanghai United Family Hospital ✉ 1139 Xianxia Lu ☎ 2216 3999, http://shanghai.ufh.com.cn; World Link Medical Centre ✉ Shanghai Centre, 1376 Nanjing Xilu ☎ 6279 7688, www.worldlink-shanghai.com; Sino-Canadian Dental Center ✉ Ninth People's Hospital, 639 Zhizao Julu ☎ 5307 5249; Shanghai Ko Sei Dental Clinic ✉ 666 Changle Lu ☎ 5404 7000.
● State hospitals: Hua Dong Hospital, Foreigners' Clinic ✉ 221 Yan'an Xilu ☎ 6248 3180, ext. 3106; Huashan Hospital, Foreigners' Clinic ✉ 12 Wulumuqi Zhonglu ☎ 5288 9999; IMCC in First People's Hospital ✉ 1878 Sichuan Beilu ☎ 5666 3031; Pediatric Hospital, Foreigners' Clinic ✉ Medical Center of Fudan University, 130 Yixue Yuanlu ☎ 6494 1990

MEDICINES

● Western medicines are available but can be expensive. If you have particular medical needs, make sure that you are equipped to satisfy them before you visit China.

MONEY MATTERS

● Money can be changed in most hotels. A passport may be required.
● Credit cards are accepted in international hotels, smart restaurants and tourist shops.
● RMB can be changed back into foreign currency when leaving China but you must produce relevant exchange receipts.

POST OFFICES

● The main post office is on the corner of Suzhou Beilu and Sichuan Beilu.
● Stamps can be purchased from most hotels.
● Post boxes are normally green; but you can hand your mail to the hotel receptionist.

TELEPHONES

● Local and long-distance calls can be made from the plentiful public phone boxes (coins or card) all over the city and from some newspaper kiosks.
● Local calls from hotel rooms are often free. International direct dialing is expensive. International calls can be made more cheaply from one of Shanghai's many telephone bars (*huaba*); phone boxes are more expensive.
● The international access code from China is 00. Or call 108 to get through to a local operator in the country being called, through whom a reverse-charge call can be made.

TIPPING

● Despite official disapproval, tipping is no longer an offense. It is now expected by tourist guides, who usually prefer money—US dollars are popular—to a gift. Hotel porters will usually accept a tip, but there is no need to tip the city's taxi drivers. In most restaurants, tips are not usually expected.

TOILETS

● Western-style toilets are common in hotels and in many restaurants, but traditional squat toilets are also widely used.
● Public toilets are not generally available and those that do exist can be distinctly unsanitary. More and better facilities are gradually appearing but you are advised to carry your own paper and soap.

TOURIST OFFICES

● Shanghai has several Tourist Information and Service Centers dotted about town, but they are of limited use and are often commercially driven. It is frequently best to ask at your hotel for local information; your concierge may equip you with a local map and make recommendations. The following Tourist Information and Service Centers are centrally located:

The Bund
✉ 5341 Zhongshan Dong 1-Lu ☎ 5321 0017 🕐 Daily 9.30–8

Jing'an Temple branch
✉ 1768 Nanjing Xilu ☎ 6248 3259 🕐 Daily 10–6

Old Town branch
✉ 149 Jiujiaochang Lu ☎ 6355 5032 🕐 Daily 9–9

Tourist hotline
☎ 962020 🕐 24 hours

Language

The official language of China is known as Mandarin in the West, or *putonghua* in China, and is based on the dialect of Beijing. It is spoken throughout China but local dialects are commonly used—the Shanghai dialect is quite different from *putonghua*. However, knowledge of a few *putonghua* words and phrases will undoubtedly be an advantage at some point.

USEFUL WORDS AND PHRASES

GREETINGS

hello/how are you	ni hao
please	qing
thank you	xiexie
goodbye	zai jian
cheers!	gan bei
no problem	mei wen ti
I'm fine	wo hen hao
My surname is...	wo xing...
I am from...	who shi laide...

IN THE HOTEL

hotel	binguan, fandian
room	fang jian
bathroom	weisheng jian

POST OFFICES, BANKS AND SHOPS

post office	youju
stamp	you piao
postcard	ming xin pian
airmail	hang kong
letter	xin
telephone	dianhua
bank	yin hang
money exchange	huan qian chu

how much?	duo shao qian?
too expensive	tai gui le
a little cheaper	pian yi dian ba
gift	li wu
credit card	xin yong ka
antique	guwu
silk	sichou
jade	yu
carpet	di tan

EATING OUT

restaurant	fan guan, fan dian, can ting
Do you have a menu in English?	You mei you ying wen cai dan?
water/cooled	shui/liang
boiled water	kaishui
coffee	kafei
black tea	hong cha
beer	pi jiu
soft drink	qi shui
rice	mi fan
fork	cha zi
knife	daozi
soup	tang

GETTING AROUND

bus	gong gong qi che
bus station	qi che zhan
boat	chuan
bicycle	zixing che
taxi	chu zu qi che
train	huo che
toilet	cesuo

HEALTH

I feel ill	wo bu shu fu
I would like	wo xiang
doctor	yi sheng
hospital	yiyuan
pharmacy	yaodian

COLORS

black	hei se
brown	he se
pink	fen hong se
red	hong se
orange	ju se
yellow	huang se
green	lu se
blue	lan se
purple	zi se
white	bai se
gold	jin se
silver	yin se
gray	hui se
turquoise	qian lan se

DAYS/MONTHS

Monday	Xing qi yi	March	san yue
Tuesday	Xing qi er	April	si yue
Wednesday	Xing qi san	May	wu yue
Thursday	Xing qi si	June	liu yue
Friday	Xing qi wu	July	qi yue
Saturday	Xing qi liu	August	ba yue
Sunday	Xing qi tian	September	jiu yue
		October	shi yue
January	yi yue	November	shi yi yue
February	er yue	December	shi er yue

USEFUL WORDS

yes	shi	why	wei shen me
no	bu	who	shei
you're welcome	bu ke qi	may I/can I	Wo ke yi/wo neng
excuse me!	dui bu qi	open	kai
where	zai na li	closed	guan bi
here	zher	church	jiao tang
there	nar	museum	bo wu guan
when	shen me	monument	ji nian bei
	shi hou	palace	gong dian

NUMBERS

0	ling	16	shi liu
1	yi	17	shi qi
2	er	18	shi ba
3	san	19	shi jiu
4	si	20	er shi
5	wu	21	er shi yi
6	liu	30	san shi
7	qi	40	si shi
8	ba	50	wu shi
9	jiu	60	liu shi
10	shi	70	qi shi
11	shi yi	80	ba shi
12	shi er	90	jiu shi
13	shi san	100	yi bai
14	shi si	1,000	yi qian
15	shi wu	million	bai wan

PRONUNCIATION

The modern phonetic romanized form of Chinese is called "pinyin". It is largely pronounced as written, but note the following:

a as in car
c as in bits when an initial consonant
e as in her
i as in feet unless preceded by c, ch, r, s, sh, z, sh, when it becomes er as in her
j as in gin
o as in ford
q like the ch in chin
s as in simple
u as in oo in cool
w as in wade, though pronounced by some as v
x like the sh in sheep, with the s given greater emphasis
y as in yoyo
z as ds in lids; zh as j in jam

ENGLISH

English is widely spoken in five-star hotels and in places where foreigners congregate. In general, however, you will find that little English is spoken. A major exception is young people, who learn English at school; many of them speak at least a moderate amount of English and a growing number of young professionals are fluent.

Timeline

THE GANGSTERS

Prewar Shanghai was an iniquitous place, fully deserving of its sobriquet as the "whore of the Orient." Nothing illustrates this better than the roles played by the gangsters, Pockmarked Huang (Huang Jinrong) and Big-eared Du (Du Yuesheng), who ran protection rackets, organized drug smuggling and controlled the city's many prostitutes. Du would warn the targets of his protection rackets of the dangers of Shanghai life by delivering a coffin to their door; Huang enjoyed perfect immunity—he was also Chief Detective for the French Sûreté.

1300s The trading center of Shanghai becomes a county seat under the jurisdiction of Jiangsu Province.

1553 The people of Shanghai build a city wall during the Ming dynasty (1368–1644) to protect them from Japanese pirates.

1842 The Opium Wars reach Shanghai, which is sacked by the British. The Treaty of Nanking, signed in August, permits them to undertake unlimited trade (Concessions), in Shanghai and four other coastal cities.

1863 The British and American Concessions merge to form the International Settlement; the French Concession remains autonomous. The foreign community enjoys "extraterritoriality," which places it outside Chinese law.

1911 The Qing dynasty falls and China becomes a republic. In 1912, the city walls are demolished to create more space.

1917 Refugees from the Russian Revolution bring a new style to Shanghai entertainment— with outrageous cabarets. Shanghai emerges as the "whore of the Orient."

1927 Chiang Kai Shek is permitted by the foreign community to move troops against the Communists through the Concessions. On April 12, the Nationalists attack the Communists in Zhabei, killing 20 and arresting several hundred, including Zhou En Lai.

Below left to right: Exterior of the Museum of the First Chinese Communist Party Congress; a display in the Shanghai Museum of Chinese History; a bust of Soong Qing-Ling; Mao and revolutionaries on badges at Dongtai Antiques Market; detail of a bronze plaque celebrating the Communist liberation of the city, at the Customs House on the Bund

NEED TO KNOW TIMELINE

1930s Japan occupies Shanghai and remains in power until the end of World War II.

1949 Mao becomes leader of the People's Republic of China and Communist troops enter Shanghai. Few foreigners remain.

1966 The Cultural Revolution begins and Shanghai, China's most industrialized and politically radical city, is the first to enter the fray. Violent rebel groups roam the streets.

1972 The Shanghai Communiqué is signed between China and the US in the Jin Jiang Hotel, signifying the end of China's isolation from the outside world.

1976 Mao dies. The Gang of Four make the city their base in their attempt to seize power.

1990s Shanghai re-enters the industrial world, becoming an autonomous municipality. Pudong is declared a Special Economic Zone, where free trade is allowed.

2008 The colossal Shanghai World Financial Center is completed (▷ 94).

2009 The Waibaidu Bridge (▷ 56–57) is returned to its place at the north end of the Bund after being removed for renovations.

2014 The Shanghai Tower, China's tallest building and the world's second-tallest, is topped out (▷ 94).

THE GANG OF FOUR

All four members of the so-called Gang of Four, who tried to seize power following the death of Chairman Mao, had Shanghai connections. Jiang Qing, Mao's last wife, was a Shanghai actress. Chang Chun Qiao had been a journalist and director of propaganda in Shanghai. Yao Wen Yuan had been editor of the newspaper *Shanghai Liberation Army Daily*. Wang Hong Wen had been a Shanghai worker and founder member of the Shanghai Workers Revolutionary Headquarters.

WORLD EXPO

Just two years after Beijing hosted the 2008 Olympics, China staged its first world's fair, Expo 2010, on a huge site straddling the Huangpu River (▷ 100–101). The six-month fair was attended by 73 million people, a record for any World Expo.

NEED TO KNOW TIMELINE

Index

INDEX

Shanghai 25 Best

WRITTEN BY Christopher Knowles
ADDITIONAL WRITING BY George McDonald
UPDATED BY Peter Ellegard
SERIES EDITOR Clare Ashton
COVER DESIGN Chie Ushio, Yuko Inagaki
DESIGN WORK Tracey Freestone, Nick Johnston
IMAGE RETOUCHING AND REPRO Ian Little

© AA MEDIA LIMITED 2015 (registered office: Fanum House, Basing View, Basingstoke, Hampshire RG21 4EA, registered number 06112600).

Published in the United Kingdom by AA Publishing

ISBN 978-1-1018-7934-4

FOURTH EDITION

SPECIAL SALES
This book is available for special discounts for bulk purchases for sales promotions or premiums. For more information, email specialmarkets@randomhouse.com.

Color separation by AA Digital Department
Printed and bound by Leo Paper Products, China

10 9 8 7 6 5 4 3 2 1

A05260
Maps in this title produced from mapping © MAIRDUMONT / Falk Verlag 2013
Transport map © Communicarta Ltd, UK

The Automobile Association would like to thank the following photographers, companies and picture libraries for their assistance in the preparation of this book.

2/18t AA/G D R Clements; 4t AA/G D R Clements; 5 AA/I Morejohn; 6cl AA/A Mockford & N Bonetti; 6cc AA/G D R Clements; 6cr AA/D Henley; 6bl AA/A Mockford & N Bonetti; 6bc AA/A Mockford & N Bonetti; 6br AA/A Mockford & N Bonetti; 7cl AA/G D R Clements; 7ccl AA/G D R Clements; 7ccr AA/G D R Clements; 7cr AA/G D R Clements; 7bl Paul Lee / Alamy; 7bc AA/A Mockford & N Bonetti; 7br AA/A Mockford & N Bonetti; 10t AA/G D R Clements; 10c AA/G D R Clements; 10/11c AA/G D R Clements; 10/11b AA/G D R Clements; 11t AA/A Mockford & N Bonetti; 11c AA/G D R Clements; 13t AA/A Mockford & N Bonetti; 13ct AA/A Mockford & N Bonetti; 13c AA/A Mockford & N Bonetti; 13bc AA/C Sawyer; 13b AA/G D R Clements; 14t AA/A Mockford & N Bonetti; 14tc AA/A Mockford & N Bonetti; 14bc AA/A Kouprianoff; 14b AA/A Mockford & N Bonetti; 15 AA/G D R Clements; 16t AA/A Mockford & N Bonetti; 16tc AA/A Mockford & N Bonetti; 16bc AA/A Mockford & N Bonetti; 16b AA/D Henley; 17t AA/G D R Clements; 17c AA/A Mockford & N Bonetti; 17b Licensed © Robin Whalley / Alamy; 18tc AA/G D R Clements; 18c AA/G D R Clements; 18cb AA/A Mockford & N Bonetti; 18b AA/A Mockford & N Bonetti; 19(I) AA/G D R Clements; 19(II) AA/A Mockford & N Bonetti; 19(III) AA/A Mockford & N Bonetti; 19(IV) AA/G D R Clements; 19(V) AA/G D R Clements; 19(VI) AA/A Mockford & N Bonetti; 19(VII) AA/G D R Clements; 20/1 AA/G D R Clements; 24l AA/A Mockford & N Bonetti; 24tr AA/A Mockford & N Bonetti; 24cr AA/A Mockford & N Bonetti; 25t Damian Harper; 25bl AA/A Mockford & N Bonetti; 25br AA/A Mockford & N Bonetti; 26l AA/G D R Clements; 26c AA/G D R Clements; 26r AA/G D R Clements; 27l AA/G D R Clements; 27r AA/G D R Clements; 28l Damian Harper; 28r Damian Harper; 29l AA/G D R Clements; 29r AA/G D R Clements; 30t AA/A Mockford & N Bonetti; 30bl AA/A Mockford & N Bonetti; 31t AA/G D R Clements; 31c AA/A Mockford & N Bonetti; 32 AA/A Mockford & N Bonetti; 33 AA/A Mockford & N Bonetti; 36l AA/A Mockford & N Bonetti; 36r Damian Harper; 37l AA/A Mockford & N Bonetti; 37r AA/A Mockford & N Bonetti; 38l AA/A Mockford & N Bonetti; 38/9 Licensed © Kevin Foy/Alamy; 39t Licensed © Tibor Bognar / Alamy; 39bl Kevin Foy / Alamy; 39br © Kevin Foy/Alamy; 40-41 TRAVEL by VISION / Alamy; 41t AA/A Mockford & N Bonetti; 41b Damian Harper; 42l AA/G D R Clements; 42tr AA/A Mockford & N Bonetti; 42br AA/G D R Clements; 43t AA/G D R Clements; 43bl AA/A Mockford & N Bonetti; 43br AA/A Mockford & N Bonetti; 44l AA/A Mockford & N Bonetti; 44r AA/A Mockford & N Bonetti; 45t AA/A Mockford & N Bonetti; 45bl Photolibrary Group; 45br AA/G D R Clements; 46 AA/A Mockford & N Bonetti; 47 AA; 48/9 AA/I Morejohn; 50 AA/A Kouprianoff; 51 AA; 52 AA/A Mockford & N Bonetti; 53 AA/A Mockford & N Bonetti; 56l Licensed © Robert Harding Picture Library Ltd / Alamy; 56r Paul Harris onasia; 57t AA/G D R Clements; 57bl Jesper Haynes onasia; 57br Paul Harris onasia; 58l AA/A Mockford & N Bonetti; 58tr AA/A Mockford & N Bonetti; 58/9b AA/A Mockford & N Bonetti; 59t AA/A Mockford & N Bonetti; 59bl AA/A Mockford & N Bonetti; 59br AA/A Mockford & N Bonetti; 60 AA/A Mockford & N Bonetti; 61t Helen Bohorquez / VWPics / Alamy; 61b John Kershaw / Alamy; 62l AA/A Mockford & N Bonetti; 62r AA/G D R Clements; 63t (Rights Managed) Gavin Hellier/Robert Harding; 63bl (Rights Managed) Gavin Hellier/Robert Harding; 63br AA/A Mockford & N Bonetti; 64 AA/A Mockford & N Bonetti; 65t AA/G D R Clements; 65c AA/A Mockford & N Bonetti; 66 AA/A Mockford & N Bonetti; 67 AA/A Mockford & N Bonetti; 70t AA/G D R Clements; 70b AA/G D R Clements; 70/1t AA/G D R Clements; 70/1b AA/G D R Clements; 71t AA/G D R Clements; 71b AA/G D R Clements; 72tl AA/A Mockford & N Bonetti; 72bl AA/A Mockford & N Bonetti; 72tr AA/A Mockford & N Bonetti; 72br AA/G D R Clements; 73t AA/G D R Clements; 73bl AA/G D R Clements; 73br AA/A Mockford & N Bonetti; 74l AA/G D R Clements; 74r AA/G D R Clements; 75t AA/A Mockford & N Bonetti; 75bl AA/A Mockford & N Bonetti; 75br AA/G D R Clements; 76t AA/A Mockford & N Bonetti; 76bl AA/A Mockford & N Bonetti; 76br AA/A Mockford & N Bonetti; 77 AA/A Mockford & N Bonetti; 78t ; 79t AA/A Mockford & N Bonetti; 80 AA/A Mockford & N Bonetti; 81 AA/G D R Clements; 84l AA/A Mockford & N Bonetti; 84r AA/A Mockford & N Bonetti; 85 AA/A Mockford & N Bonetti; 86l AA/G D R Clements; 86r AA/G D R Clements; 87t AA/A Mockford & N Bonetti; 87b AA/A Mockford & N Bonetti; 88 AA/A Mockford & N Bonetti; 89 AA/A Mockford & N Bonetti; 92 Dan Yeger / Alamy; 93t imageBROKER / Alamy; 93b Paul Lee / Alamy; 94r AA/A Mockford & N Bonetti; 94l AA/A Mockford & N Bonetti; 95t AA/A Mockford & N Bonetti; 95b AA/A Mockford & N Bonetti; 96t AA/G D R Clements; 96c AA/A Mockford & N Bonetti; 97 AA/G D R Clements; 100tl Xinhua / Alamy; 100bl Xinhua / Alamy; 100-101 Xinhua / Alamy; 102tl AA/A Kouprianoff; 102tr AA/A Kouprianoff; 102bl AA/G D R Clements; 102br AA/G D R Clements; 103t AA/G D R Clements; 103b AA/A Kouprianoff; 104l AA/G D R Clements; 104r AA/G D R Clements; 105-106t Panoramic Images/Robert Harding; 107 AA/A Mockford & N Bonetti; 108/9t AA/C Sawyer; 108tr AA/A Mockford & N Bonetti; 108tcr AA; 108cbr AA/G D R Clements; 108br AA/G D R Clements; 110/112 AA/C Sawyer; 113 AA/A Mockford & N Bonetti; 114/125 AA/A Mockford & N Bonetti; 124bl AA/A Mockford & N Bonetti; 124br AA/G D R Clements; 125bl AA/G D R Clements; 125bc AA/A Mockford & N Bonetti; 125br AA/A Mockford & N Bonetti

Every effort has been made to trace the copyright holders, and we apologise in advance for any accidental errors. We would be happy to apply the corrections in the following edition of this publication.

TITLES IN THE SERIES